GALLEON CLAN ESCRIMA

THE JOURNEY OF SINAWALI

JOSEPH L. GALLEON

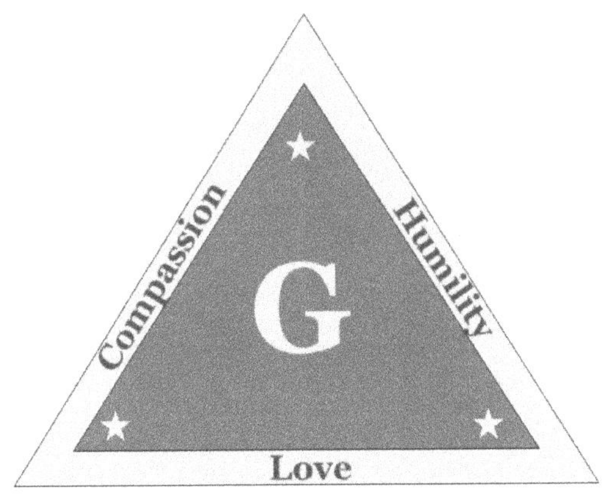

Houston Martial Arts Media

Dedication

I dedicate this book to my father, Gaudioso (George) Daguman Galleon (1898-1970). My father came from Massin, Leyte, Philippines in 1920 after honorably serving in the U. S. Navy during WWI. He was able to migrate to the U. S. after passing basic English speaking and writing skills exams along with basic knowledge of American history and memorizing the U.S. Constitution. He settled in Pasadena, California. Fifteen years after immigrating to the U.S. he was granted U.S. citizenship in 1935.

Table of Contents

GALLEON CLAN ESCRIMA

THE JOURNEY OF SINAWALI DOUBLE-WEAPON FIGHTING

JOSEPH L. GALLEON

FOREWORD

Jason Evans

It is a great honor to be asked to write the foreword for this book. I have known Guro Joe for over 17 years and in that time, he has become more than a teacher to me. He has become my training partner, mentor, and more importantly, my friend. Guro Joe has authored this book to preserve his family legacy and the family system of Escrima his father passed down to him and his brothers. Most Filipino martial arts are family or tribal arts, passed down from generation to generation and the Galleon Clan System of Escrima is no different. Guro Joe started his journey in his family system when he was 6 years old. He decided to gift the world with his family art by sharing it with his students, those outside of his family. I am fortunate enough to be one of the first students to whom he started teaching. His dedication and love for the martial art shows through in his teaching and the knowledge he passes on to his students.

I started learning Filipino martial arts from Guro Joe in 2006 and from the first time he showed me his family system, I was hooked. The combination of beauty and effectiveness that shown through in each aspect of the system made it easy to want to learn. Very few people have been exposed to the Galleon Clan system of Escrima in the United States. Guro Joe lives in Houston, Texas and that is where he started sharing his family art and continues to share it with his students today.

This book covers the Lakbay Sinawali principles, concepts, techniques, and drills within Galleon Clan Escrima. The Galleon Clan System of Escrima is a complete and comprehensive Filipino martial arts system comprised of double blade (Sinawali), single blade (Espada), staff (Sibat), blade and knife (Espada y Daga), knife (Daga), and empty hand (Pangamot) fighting. All concepts and principles within the sinawali subset can be seen throughout the rest of Galleon Clan Escrima. The way everything is built off of the sinawali subset makes learning this art one where techniques, drills, and play can be woven in and out of seemingly seamlessly.

Guro Joe has dedicated his life to learning, training, and sharing martial arts. For him to be the first to share his family art to those outside his family is a tremendous thing and no small matter that should be overlooked. The history, culture, and knowledge passed down through Guro Joe from what his father passed down to him is a treasure that should be documented and shared with the world. This is exactly what he is doing with the writing of this book. He is sharing the sinawali subset of Galleon Clan Escrima within the pages of this book. This book will make a powerful addition to any martial artists library.

Chapter One

Introduction

Every tribal group and family clan in the Philippines has a system of Escrima and Lakbay Sinawali techniques. Their own interpretations of these interweaving Sinawali techniques can vary from village to village and from family clan to family clan as well as their explanation of these techniques. The "Galleon Clan" techniques explained here-in is material related and taught to me from my late father Gaudioso "George" Daguman Galleon, (1898-1970) a Visayan Filipino from the Island of Leyte, in the district of Massin. After serving in the U.S. Navy during WWI, my father immigrated to the United States in 1920. He settled in Pasadena, California, where he and my mother raised six children, of which I am the youngest.

Being the youngest of six children, my father did not want to teach me the art as he did with my older brothers because during WWII there had been much death and destruction. He only wanted to live a peaceful life with his family. When I came home from my first day of school when I was six years old, I was crying and had a black eye and bloody nose, my clothes were torn and dirty. My father and mother consoled me and wanted to know what happened and what caused this to occur. I told them some boys jumped me and started beating me up as I was walking home from school and did not know any of them. After that my father said, "Son, you need to know how to fight and take care of yourself." So, my introduction to Escrima began. Being only six, my father could not train me as an adult, so first I was taught simple "Cinco Tero" and "Arco" drills, as well as basic "Pangamot," or barehanded fighting, and basic "Sikaran," or kicking drills similar to karate.

What fascinated me about Escrima was "Sinawali" and how simple techniques can be interwoven together to create complex patterns with either a single weapon or double weapons. I realized this when a friend of my father's, Mr. Hipolito, from the Philippines, and now lived in Los Angeles, CA, would visit. My father met Mr. Hipolito while attending Sunday Mass at St. Andrews Catholic Church. Mr. Hipolito was visiting his daughter, who lived in Pasadena. Mr. Hipolito, who was a kind man, introduced himself to my father and said he was a Grandmaster of Escrima. He heard my father was a good "Escrimador," and he needed a good training partner. Usually, Mr. Hipolito would come over to our house on Saturday afternoons, so he and my father could train in the backyard. As a young boy, I was amazed to see them engage in double Sinawali patterns using either swords or sticks as they called techniques out, on the fly, so to speak. This book is based on those memories of Sinawali training using those techniques, patterns, and drills. The last chapter in this book is a list of ten (10) line drills simulating and emulating, from my memory, the Sinawali drills and patterns my father would perform with Mr. Hipolito in our backyard.

Please note that the "Galleon Clan" is a large family clan that still exists within the Philippines today and includes family members from the Islands of Cebu, Leyte, Bohol, and Luzon as well. Additionally, Galleon Clan has spread throughout the world as family clan members immigrate to various countries around the world seeking professional job opportunities for themselves in medicine, engineering, IT industry, accounting, banking, finance, and law.

Below is the second sub-system of Escrima on Lakbay Sinawali from the "Galleon Clan" system of Escrima. Please note that these techniques are the personal opinions and teachings of my late father George D. Galleon and, as stated before, may be different from other family or tribal systems.

Since Escrima is taught in many family clans and in various tribal systems, many of these techniques may be similar in nature to a seasoned practitioner. The reason for such similarities is because a strike, a slash, a thrust, and a parry are all similar in all systems. Even in Western fencing techniques, the same is true. For example, in the several styles of "Karate," a kick is a kick, and a punch is a punch. This rule applies in Escrima, but the interpretation of each application and the principles may be different from system to system. Like "Karate," all styles are good and have their specific application. No one system can claim to be the best because all styles and systems of Escrima have a specific application to a given principle, philosophy, or technique. All systems are good and have a valid practical application that we can all learn from to explore and grow in knowledge and understanding to achieve wisdom. Wisdom only comes through knowledge and experience, from time and practice, sparring, actual combat, and teaching. If through experience, growth, and understanding one produces new, valid techniques that work for that individual, it is truly a valid application for that individual. It does not mean that it is not good because it is new. If it works, do it and explore your capabilities. This is the philosophy of the late martial artist Bruce Lee, who after studying various fighting styles all around the world, developed his own way, or style, known as JKD that was personally suited for him. This should be the same philosophy for all martial art students and practitioners of Escrima.

The material contained in this book is only a practical guideline to follow. The "Lakbay Sinawali" techniques in this book are the foundation techniques that can be arranged into numerous prefix and suffix patterns that one can experiment with to develop new patterns to suit one's abilities. The practitioner is encouraged to go off exploring and finding out what works for himself/herself, apply those techniques, and develop them into his/her natural way. We all have different body types, ages, weight and physical capabilities that we must explore in order to achieve enlightenment for ourselves. However, that does not mean that we just reach a certain level and stop; we must continue to grow and learn to understand why certain techniques are executed and performed that way, for there is a practical application to any given technique in any system. This will insure us that once we have the foundation laid correctly, we will start to grow and develop into a high level of martial art proficiency.

As you study the drills in this book on "Lakbay Sinawali" techniques, you will notice that there are no disarming techniques described in this book. The reason for this is because my late father never believed that disarming techniques really work effectively in a double-bladed weapon system of equal length, weight, and design style. The speed of the bladed weapons is too fast for anyone to foolishly step in and try to execute a disarm technique. The 10 line drills or "Entablados" do have disarming techniques within each one listed in Chapter 8. The disarming techniques are placed in them to familiarize the student with basic disarming "Snake," Vine," and "Hook" disarming techniques. But, the philosophy of my father was don't attempt to execute a disarming technique, but to only "defang the snake." His reasons were obvious for he would simply execute a "Sonkete" or "Picado" poke or thrust with his other weapon while you were attempting to execute a disarm. He would also explain the fallacy of attempting a disarm in a double weapon system. Remember, "Entablado" is only a two-partner structured pattern drill that has combat techniques in them to practice or to show off your skills in a performance before or during a Escrima tournament.

My father's beliefs were that it is best to "defang the snake," so to speak with either a "Crusada Abierta" or "Crusada Cerrada" gunting/scissor blocking technique. To "defang the snake," one weapon either parries your opponent's weapon or strikes a target area of your opponent while with the other weapon you strike your opponent's hand. With this type of technique, your opponent's weapon will naturally drop and fall to the ground or floor, disarming the weapon.

My father taught me disarming techniques like the Vine, Snake, and Punyo disarms. Additionally, he taught me Cadena quick release disarms, but only applied them to a stick art, not to a bladed art. In most systems when learning disarming techniques, your training partner will let you perform and execute the disarming techniques. With time and practice, they are very easy to execute and perform. However, in a real combat confrontation, your opponent will do everything in his/her power for you to not even get in close, much less try to execute a disarm technique.

If it is your desire to have the ability to execute clean disarming techniques, it is best to have your training partner do everything with his skill to disrupt you from executing a clean disarming technique. You will find out quickly that it is exceedingly difficult to execute a disarm technique cleanly without being exposed to a counterattack, especially in a double-bladed art. Escrima is extremely fast with rapid striking patterns followed with offbeat timing and snapping strikes. In addition, there are attacks by drawing and faking, which make it an art that a practitioner must practice throughout his/her lifetime; it is not easy to master. If you have ever seen live blades demonstrations at martial arts performances or seminars, you have noticed that each performer highly respects the live blade and plays the art in a respectful "Larga" or "Larga Mano" long range distance. They never rush in to perform a disarm technique and there is good reason - a sword has length and is mainly for distance fighting.

I believe that too many FMA organizations today have incorporated close range stick fighting as well as Filipino Kuntao Silat close quarters empty hands techniques into the bladed art, which to me is not very practical while using live bladed weapons. It is too easy to expose oneself to a counterattack while engaging in close quarters fighting range.

So, with that out of the way, it is the purpose of this book to only instruct you in the fighting techniques of "Lakbay Sinawali," as interpreted by the "Galleon Clan," as a double-bladed art form. Due to disarming techniques being a different training method, it would require several additional chapters in this book to try to explain the complexities of disarming.

For now, just remember to "defang the snake" at long to middle range, and your opponent's weapon will drop. You will also notice that when practicing a set form, or Sumbrada, using these Lakbay Sinawali techniques, it is possible to break into a free style sparring session.

You will notice that you cannot do the techniques as described in this book; you can only execute a small fraction of the total Sinawali routine. The reason for that is because full contact sparring simulates a real combat fighting scenario. Your training partner is constantly moving and positioning himself/herself, delivering and executing multiple successions of strikes, and attacks either by combinations, drawing, and faking in rapid succession.

Don't be discouraged for not being able to complete a Lakbay Sinawali technique during a full contact sparring session. You will soon notice with experience in full contact sparring, one must quickly rebound from an attack, parry or block, and attempt another technique. As a result, you can only use a small fraction of that technique that you want to apply. You might say to yourself, "Why learn these complicated Lakbay Sinawali techniques any way, if I can only use a small fraction of them at any given time in a full contact sparring session or tournament play?" The most important reason is because Lakbay Sinawali techniques teach you to move your weapons in rapid succession into interweaving patterns without getting your hands or weapons tied up or in a locked position. Lakbay Sinawali techniques and routines give you the foundation and knowledge to use whatever technique, or part of a technique, at any given time to attack and strike your opponent with a multitude of various combinations of striking patterns in a full contact sparring session or tournament play.

It is just like practicing Karate Do Katas. You never fight an opponent in Karate using a complete Kata routine; you only use a small fraction of a striking technique that exist in a Kata. The same is true in Escrima. The complete Lakbay Sinawali routines are performed like Karate Do Katas for practice and stage performances to demonstrate one's skill, proficiency, and level of accomplishment in that art. This form of presentation or stage performance is called "Entablado" in Escrima, and it is a display of one's proficiency, skill, and level of expertise. It can be performed as a solo "Carenza" performance or as a two person "Sombrada."

CHAPTER TWO

Sinawali Expressions

Abanico – means "Fan" and is romantically used by Filipinos in Escrima for defensive blocking by using a quick wrist action to execute the defensive block from side to side or a circular motion around the head. Sometimes it is referred to as "sinalakot," which comes from the "Tagalog" word "Salakot," it is the conical shaped agricultural field hat, or sombrero, used in the Philippines Islands and other Asian countries. Also, romantically it is referred to as "Volara la Cometa," or "Fly the Comet," due to wheeling your weapon around your head like a helicopter blade.

Abierta or Abierto – means "Open."

Arnis – a Chabacano word that comes from the Spanish word **"Arnes,"** which means armor. **"Arnis de Mano"** means "armor of the hand," but it is referring to hands as a weapon, or empty hands fighting. It also refers to fighting without the use of a weapon, which is also known as **"Panantukan."** This will only occur when one loses one's weapon, or weapons, and must fight empty handed. This technique may also incorporate the use of the elbows, knees, feet, take downs, and ground fighting in general, which is known as **"Dumog."** The expression **"Filipino Arnis"** is in reference to the martial arts as a whole that are practiced in the Philippines Islands.

Baguhan – a Sinawali technique, like an **"Abecedario 6,"** but means novice or beginner. It is a technique that has an awkward looking execution of the strike and has a romantic meaning of beginner because of the awkwardness of the strike. The Chabacano and Spanish word for this is **"Novicio,"** which means beginner.

Bagsak Sak-Sak – means to "Drop and Thrust," or sometimes known as **"Bagsak-Salot,"** because one also lowers the shoulder of the weapon hand while executing this technique.

Bunot Kaluban – means "drawing of the sword(s)" or pulling one's sword out to fight. The Sinawali technique of "Bunot Kaluban" is the action of drawing the swords back in opposite directions to execute a double cut. In Chabacano and Spanish it is called **"Tirada de las Espaldas."** In the Galleon Clan system, it is drawing out the sword(s) to deliver the No. 12 strike called "tero grave", which is also used by other "Visayan" tribal systems.

Cadena Real – means **"Royal Chain,"** which has reference to a technique of blocking or placing one's weapon against the opponent's weapon and pivots one's weapon against the opponent's weapon as you parry rotate over while executing a strike to the opponent or rebounding to the opposite side of your opponent. It is used in a style of Escrima known as "Estilo De Cuerdas."

Combate Adentro – means inside or close-range fighting. It is also known as **"estancia corto"**.

Cerrada – means **"Closed."**

Crusada Cerrada – a crosscut strike by using either the right weapon over the left weapon or the left weapon over the right weapon and is executed in a rapid motion at any angle and at any height. It is also used in **"Suffixing"** to augment a strike pattern or Sinawali routine.

De Cadena – means **"Unchain"** and has reference to empty hands trapping and striking in quick rapid movements, as well as, with the use of a weapon. It refers to quickly chaining, or placing one's weapon against the opponent's weapon, and unchaining, or releasing one's weapon to the other side for a parry and strike. This technique is sometimes called **"Cadena Decadena,"** or chain and unchain.

Estrella – means "Star" in Chabacano and Spanish. It has a romantic reference to any block or parry against a weapon at 90°, like a cross block or like an inside block, which is called **"Estrella Cerrada."** An outside block is called **"Estrella Abierta."**

Kali Escrima – The art was called **"Kali"** before the coming of the Spanish and Christianity to the Philippines Islands. **"Kali"** means blade or sword in many of the tribal dialects, and the art in general was known as **"Kali"** until the end of the 16th century. **"Escrima"** is a Chabacano and Spanish word that literally means skirmish, or fight. It is used by the Spanish and Filipinos for a sword fight or even a dueling art between two or more combatants.

Kilos-Paa – means **"Footwork"** and in Chabacano and Spanish it is called **"Paseos."**

Kambal – a Tagalog word which means **"Twin."** The Chabacano and Spanish word for this is **"Gemelo,"** and it has the Filipino romantic meaning of two of any technique in Sinawali.

Larga Mano – means **"long hand"** but has reference to long range fighting distance. It is the opposite of **"Combate Adentro."**

Langit – means **"Heaven"** in Tagalog and refers to the high line striking patterns in Sinawali, like the high line six striking pattern of **"Heaven Six."** The Chabacano and Spanish expression for this is **"Cielo Seis."**

Langit at Lupa – means **"Heaven & Earth"** in Tagalog and refers to the upper and lower combination striking patterns in Sinawali, like the six-striking pattern of **"Heaven and Earth Six,"** which is also known as **"Standard Six."** The Chabacano and Spanish expression for this is **"Cielo y Tierra Seis."**

Magbabayo – (Downward Figure Eight Strike) refers to the name of a tool that is used in the Philippines to repair the earthen dikes of rice patties; it looks like a brick layer's trowel but is smaller in size. An instructor may call out **"Magbabayo"** Downward Figure Eight Striking pattern or **"Magbabayo Invertido"** Upward Figure Eight Striking pattern. **"Salot Saboy"** is also sometimes used for an Upward Figure Eight striking pattern because it has reference to scoop and throw starting from the **"Saboy"** and **"Aldabis"** strike position.

Mano-Mano – means "**Hand to Hand**" but has reference to short range fighting distance, like **"Combate Adentro,"** but with empty hands or without the use of a weapon.

Medio or Media – means middle and has reference to middle range fighting or one half of some object.

Planchada – means **"Flatten"** but is romantically used by Filipinos in Kali or Escrima as a flat level strike parallel to the floor or ground and at any height.

Planchada Abierta – to deliver a strike from the open position, and the strike pattern travels parallel or level to the floor or ground terminating in the closed position on the opposite side.

Panastas – a Tagalog word for meeting force with force, like an inside block, or against or meeting the force. The Chabacano and Spanish word for this is **"Contra,"** which means against.

Palasut – a Tagalog word for following or going with the force, like an outside block, following with the force of the strike or even passing the strike. The Chabacano or Spanish word for this is "**Seguida**."

Planchada Cerrada – to deliver a strike from the closed position, and the strike pattern travels parallel or level to the floor or ground terminating in the open position on the opposite side.

Redonda or Redondo – a Chabacano or Spanish word that means region, area, zone or round but is used romantically by Filipinos in Escrima as a circular motion like **"Abanico,"** however, one's weapon travels in a complete 360° circular motion before striking its intended target at any angle or height.

Salot Saboy – upward six Striking Pattern, also may be referred as **"Salat Saboy,"** meaning shoulder and hip respectively, but the true meaning or the romantic Filipino reference as applied to Escrima is **"Scoop and Throw."** Just picture yourself scooping in a bag of seeds hanging at your hips, getting the seeds in your hand, and launching them into the air in an upward direction across your upper body. The Chabacano or Spanish expression for this is **"achicada y tirada"** or **"achicada y echada."**

Suffixing – to add something at the end of something. An example of this is the word "quick." By adding the suffix ending "ly," now becomes "quickly." The true Filipino meaning in Escrima, suffixing refers to adding or augmenting some other technique at the end of a technique or sinawali routine as a transition into another sinawali technique. The Chabacano or Spanish expressions for this are **"aumentar," "aumenta," "aumentara," "aumentada,"** or **"anadir," "anadiese,"** or **"anade"** or even **"sufijo"** or **"sufijada".** Sometimes this technique is even called **"prefixing"** or **"Prefiada,"** but in general it is known as **"Suffixing"** in English and **"Sufijo"** or **"Sufijada"** in Chabacano or Spanish.

Sombrada – sometimes spelled **"Sumbrada,"** means shaded or shadowed and is used by Filipinos in Escrima for a **"Roof Block"** as well as in sinawali routines where two practitioners use the same striking pattern techniques in mirror image of each other, like shadow boxing. It comes from the Spanish verb **"Sombrear,"** which means to shadow or to shade and has a different spelling in Chabacano.

Tero – means strike in Chabacano, and it comes for the Old Spanish word **"Tiro"** it is also known as **"Armarra"** in Tagalog" or **"Golpe"** in modern Spanish.

CHAPTER THREE

Salutes

In this chapter we cover the salutes in the Galleon Clan System of Escrima.

The salute is to be performed when starting class, ending class, and before beginning a partner drill or single person demonstration. There are three salutes, each for the different type of weapon being held or with empty hands at the time of saluting. The salute is based off the term "Maharlika," which means freedom or free class. It is the salute of the warrior class. These salutes are a sign of respect for the art.

Empty Hand Salute (Maharlika)

Starting in a "neutral" position with the feet together, raise your hands to the center of your chest. Put your right hand in a fist and cover it with your left hand. Your elbows should be slightly pointing toward the ground with your hands out away from your chest. From here, you will lean forward, bending at the waist. Make sure your eyes are looking up and forward as you bow in the salute. You do not want to look at the ground, you want to maintain eyeline of your surroundings in front of you.

Single Blade/Stick Salute (Maharlika)

Starting in a "neutral" position with your feet together, raise your hands to the center of your chest. Put your right hand, which should be holding a single weapon such as a stick or blade, in a fist and cover it with your left hand. Your elbows should be slightly pointing toward the ground with your hands out away from your chest. From here, you will lean forward, bending at the waist. Make sure your eyes are looking up and forward as you bow in the salute. You do not want to look at the ground, you want to maintain eyeline of your surroundings in front of you.

Double Blade/Stick Salute (Triangle)

Starting in a "neutral" position with your feet together, gripping a blade or stick in each hand, raise your hands to chest height. The weapons should be crossed at the centerline in front of you forming the two top portions of a triangle. Your elbows should be slightly pointing toward the ground with your hands away from your chest. From here, you will lean forward as you bow in the salute. You do not want to be looking at the ground, you want to maintain eyeline of your surroundings in front of you.

 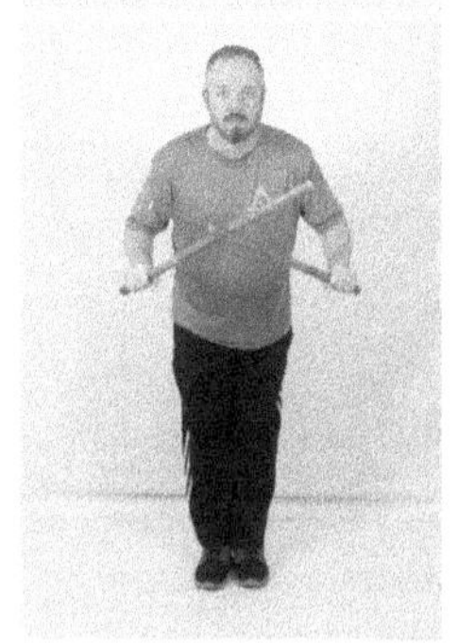

Footwork Patterns

There are many footwork patterns in Escrima. Described below are the footwork patterns utilized in my family system. There are other footwork patterns used, but these are the main ones. Each technique and drill can be performed using the any of the footwork patterns as described below. It is encouraged to practice the techniques using the various patterns in order to become familiar and comfortable with sparring when the need or occasion arises to switch footwork.

Female Triangle

The female triangle is an open, or "Abierta," footwork patter that utilizes stepping forward in a 45-degree angle with either your right or left foot. Standing in a "neutral" stance with your feet together you step out with your right foot 45-degrees while maintaining your left foot in the "neutral" position. Using replacement footwork, step with your left foot out 45-degrees even with your right foot and return your right foot to the "neutral" position. You can also rhythmically swing, or "Columpia," back and forth between right and left foot lead, returning the opposite foot to the "neutral" position.

Male Triangle

The Male Triangle is a closed, or "Cerrada," footwork pattern that utilizes stepping back with your left or right foot at a 45-degree angle. Standing in a "neutral" stance with your feet together you step back with your left foot 45-degrees while maintaining your right foot in the "neutral" position. Using replacement footwork, step with your left foot back to neutral, as soon as your left foot lands, quickly step back 45 degrees with your right foot. You can also rhythmically swing, or "Columpia," back and forth between right and left foot lead, returning the opposite foot to the "neutral" position.

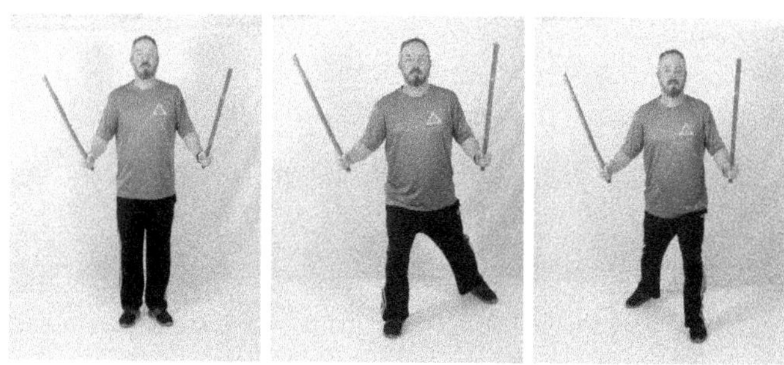

Offline Sidestep

Offline Sidestepping is a footwork pattern to get you offline of your opponent and their attack while maintaining your forward positioning and keeping you oriented to where you can still block or counter their attack. You begin by stepping forward in a 45-degree angle with either your right or left foot. Standing in a "neutral" stance with your feet together you step out with your right foot 45-degrees while swinging your left foot directly behind your right foot with your toes pointing perpendicular to your right foot. Standing in a "neutral" stance with your feet together you step out with your left foot 45-degrees while swinging your right foot directly behind your left foot with your toes pointing perpendicular to your left foot. You can also rhythmically swing, or "Columpia," back and forth between right and left foot lead, returning the opposite foot directly behind the forward foot.

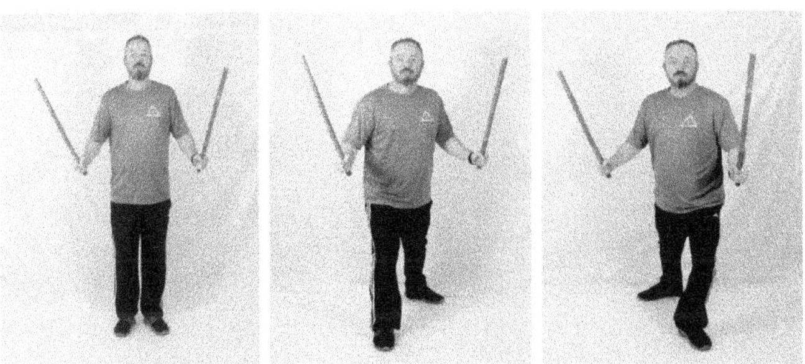

Offline 45 Degrees

Offline Sidestepping to 45 degrees is a footwork pattern to get you offline of your opponent and their attack while positioning you to be oriented where you can still block or counter their attack while facing them. You begin by stepping forward in a 45-degree angle with either your right or left foot. Standing in a "neutral" stance with your feet together you step out with your right foot 45-degrees while swinging your left foot behind your right foot with your toes pointing perpendicular to your right foot to where your body is facing your opponent at a 45-degree angle from where you were. Standing in a "neutral" stance with your feet together you step out with your left foot 45-degrees while swinging your right foot behind your left foot with your toes pointing perpendicular to your left foot to where your body is facing your opponent at a 45-degree angle from where you were. You can also rhythmically swing, or "Columpia," between right and left foot lead.

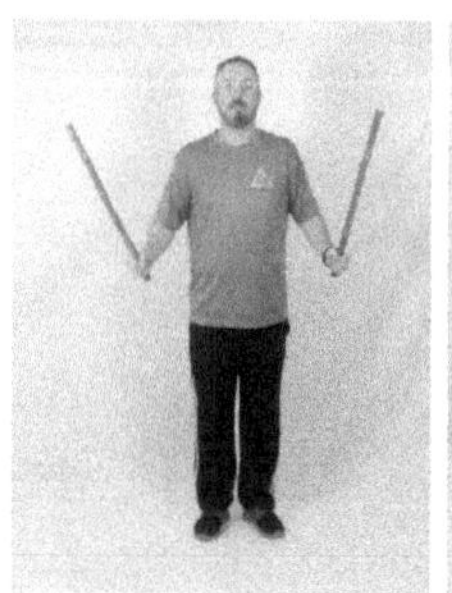  

Offline 90 Degrees

Offline Sidestepping to 90 degrees is a footwork pattern to get you offline of your opponent and their attack while positioning you to be oriented to where you can still block or counter their attack while facing their side. You begin by stepping forward in a 45-degree angle with either your right or left foot. Standing in a "neutral" stance with your feet together you step out deep with your right foot 45-degrees while swinging your left foot directly behind your right foot with your toes pointing perpendicular to your right foot to where your body is facing the side of your opponent at a 90-degree angle from where you were. Standing in a "neutral" stance with your feet together you step out deep with your left foot 45-degrees while swinging your right foot directly behind your left foot with your toes pointing perpendicular to your left foot to where your body is facing the side of your opponent at a 90-degree angle from where you were. You can also rhythmically swing, or "Columpia," back and forth between right and left foot lead, returning the opposite foot directly behind the forward foot.

Lutang

Lutang (also known as floating footwork) is a footwork pattern of moving your lead leg away from your opponent's strike or attack in a swiping or floating motion behind you without losing your forward stance. It is not an actual step back or retreat. You can "float" the foot behind you without touching the ground and bringing it right back to the front or you can let the foot touch the ground lightly before bringing it back to the front.

Cross Stepping

Cross Stepping is a footwork pattern used to gain situational advantage over your opponent by crossing your rear leg in front of your lead leg and then pivoting to end up in a position off angle of your opponent in the opposite lead. You can also step across your rear leg with your lead leg to pivot and end up in a position off angle of your opponent in the opposite lead.

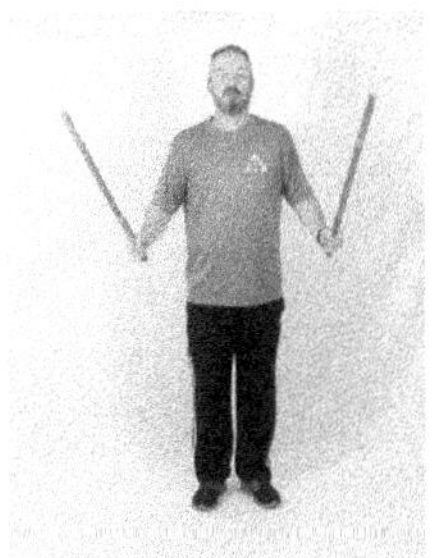

Spring Step

The Spring Step is a defensive position/action when your opponent is coming at you with a hard strike from the #12 striking position or a "Bolante" type strike. When the strike comes, you block with your weapons in a X-block or roof block manner.

While blocking the strike, step behind your lead foot with your rear foot, crouching at the knees as you accept the strike with your block. This action of accepting the strike with your block while crouching helps cushion the strike and allows you to coil your body through the crouch. By bending at the knees with the crouch, you are then able to "spring" back up powerfully going through the strike with your block and striking at the same time.

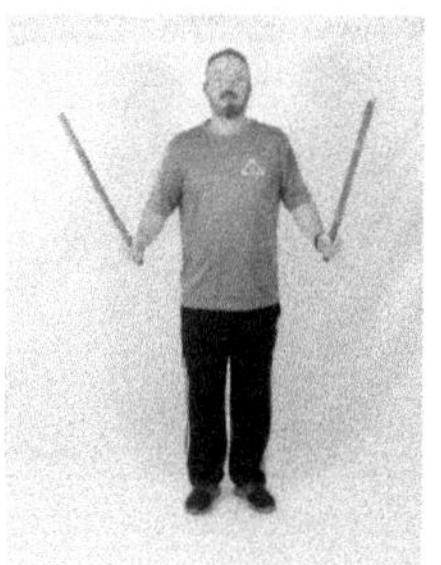  

Chapter Five

Warm-Up Exercises

It is highly recommended that a practitioner or beginner/novice to the art of "Lakbay Sinawali" always begin with these warm-up exercises to prepare and condition the body for such activity. These exercise drills will loosen up the muscles and ligaments to execute the art in an effective and speedy manner that is necessary in real combat, practice sparring conditions, or in tournament play, which is becoming more accepted and popular today than ever before.

1. Exercise Drill: "Wisik" (Wrist Twisting Motion Exercise)

Grip a baston with each hand in the medio or middle section of each baston. Then extend your arms out parallel to the ground at shoulder height. Start twisting your bastons by simply rotating your firm grip in a clockwise and counterclockwise rotating torque manner. Execute this drill thirty to sixty times rapidly. Depending on your conditioning, it is encouraged that you build up to this in time so that you can execute this drill before muscle fatigue in a one-minute time period. Then, after a short rest period, with this same twisting rotating wrist action, you will now execute this exercise by using the female triangle foot work and perform a **"Taga"** to **"Aldabis"** diagonal travel motion and back up to the beginning **"Taga"** starting position while twisting the wrist as you move down and back up. This exercise is performed or executed by alternating with each forward advancing foot work in the female triangle foot work from right foot lead stance and the left foot lead stance. Execute this exercise ten (10) times on each side. This exercise will build up your wrist to deliver fast action snap hits and later the ability to execute an advanced technique called **"Florette."** In time after you have built up your conditioning and can do this exercise very easily without any muscle fatigue, start gripping your bastons now in the "corto" position or near the "punyo" section of your bastons and execute these drills. Notice the difference between the two grips positions in muscle fatigue. In the Philippines, weapons come in various lengths, weight, sizes and style or design, so it is necessary to have good conditioning in usage of bladed weapons that exist in Filipino Arnis.

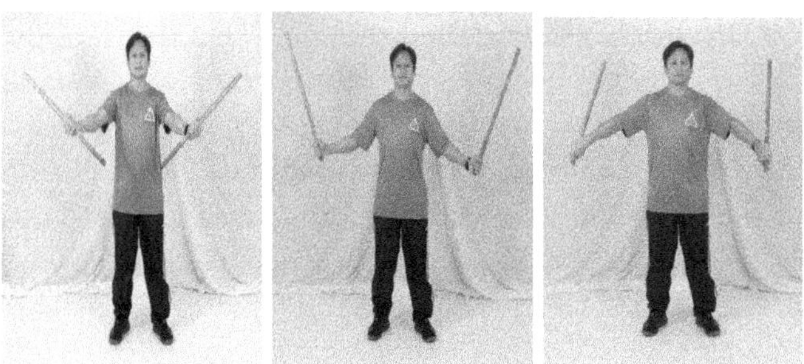

2. Exercise Drill: Wrist and Elbow Bending

While standing in a normal stance with feet shoulder width apart, grip each baston firmly near the "punyo" section, with your elbows near your side and forearms parallel to the ground and your bastons pointing upward in a vertical position. Now, begin this exercise by simply bending your elbow about 90 deg. downward and extending your wrist downward as your baston extends out, downward passed the parallel position, and then immediately return the baston back to its original position. Then, execute this bending exercise by simply alternating on the right side and immediately followed on the left side. Execute this twenty (20) to thirty (30) times. This should take about one (1) minute to complete.

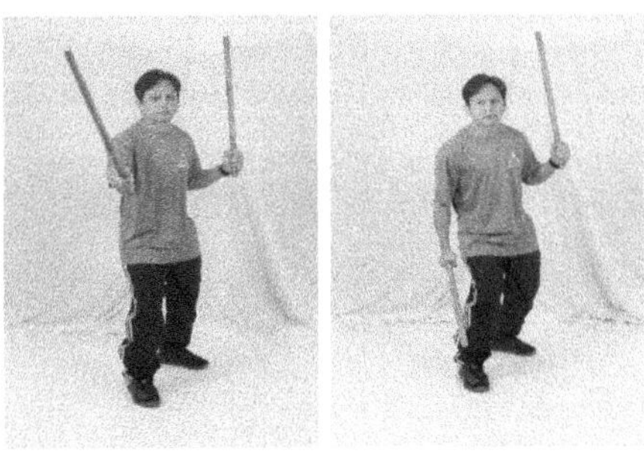

3. Exercise Drill: "Bagsak Sak-Sak" (Drop and Thrust)

This exercise is a striking technique and is performed by alternating with each forward advancing foot work from the female triangle foot work from right foot lead stance to left foot lead stance. First, step forward into a right foot lead forward advance position and execute a **"Taga"** No.1 strike to your opponent's left temple or neck and once the weapon has reached its intended strike, immediately drop cut down your opponent's body down to the center line midsection and execute a No.5 **"Sak-Sak"** up to the heart. Then, pull your weapon out by rotating your wrist counterclockwise ¼ quarter turn or with a twist of your wrist. Then execute this same technique but now from a left foot lead position and with your left-hand weapon on the right side of your opponent. Execute this exercise ten (10) times on each side by alternating on each side. This exercise will build up your ability to execute **"Bagsak Sak-Sak"** (Drop and Thrust) from any angle and from any striking pattern because in real combat, one can easily fake out your opponent by simply dropping and thrusting at any time and this really comes from a style commonly known as **"Estilo de Engano"** or style of faking.

4. Exercise Drill: "De Cuerdas Arriba"

This means to untie a high cord or string but has a Filipino Romantic meaning in **"Arnis"** of returning a high strike immediately after a descending strike: This exercise is also a striking technique and is performed or executed by alternating with each forward advancing foot work from the female triangle foot work from right foot lead stance and the left foot lead stance. First, step forward into a right foot lead forward advance position and execute a **"Taga"** No.1 strike to your opponent's left temple or neck. Once the weapon has reached its intended strike, immediately drop cut down through your opponent's body to the center line and immediately turn the cutting edge of your blade and execute a returning **"Aldabis sa Ilalim,"** which is an inside upward steep diagonal strike that is almost vertical. Execute this exercise ten (10) times on each side by alternating on each side. This exercise will build up your ability to execute returning strikes in a speedy manner.

5. Exercise Drill: "De Cuerdas Abajo"

This means to untie a bottom cord or string but has a Filipino Romantic meaning in Arnis of returning a high strike immediately after a **"Planchada Abierta"** strike: This exercise is a striking technique and is performed by alternating with each forward advancing foot work from the female triangle foot work from right foot lead stance and the left foot lead stance. First, step forward into a right foot lead forward advance position and execute a **"Planchada Abierta"** No.3 strike to your opponent's right side. Once the weapon has reached its intended strike, immediately drop cut across through your opponent's body centerline of the midsection immediately turning the cutting edge of your blade and execute a returning **"Aldabis sa Ilalim,"** which is an inside, upward steep diagonal strike that is almost vertical. Execute these ten (10) times on each side by alternating on each side. This exercise will build up your ability to execute returning strikes in a speedy manner.

6. Exercise Drill: "Abanico Bagsak Sak-Sak" (Fan with Drop and Thrust)

This exercise is a striking technique and is performed by alternating with each forward advancing foot work from the female triangle foot work from right foot lead stance and the left foot lead stance. First, step forward into a right foot lead forward advance position and execute a **"Taga"** No.1 strike to your opponent's left temple or neck. Once the weapon has reached its intended strike, immediately **"abanico"** over to the opposite side to your opponent's right temple or neck and strike with a **"Bartical"** strike. Then, immediately drop cut your opponent's body down to the center line midsection and executes a No.5 **"Sak-Sak"** up to the heart. Next, pull your weapon out by rotating your wrist counterclockwise ¼ quarter turn, or with a twist of your wrist. Then, execute this same technique but now from a left foot lead position and with your left-hand weapon on the right side of your opponent. Execute these ten (10) times on each side by alternating on each side. This exercise will build up your ability to execute **"Abanico Bagsak Sak-Sak"** (Drop and Thrust) from any angle and from any striking pattern because in real combat one can easily fake out your opponent by simply dropping and thrusting at any time. This really comes from a style commonly known as **"Estilo de Engano,"** or style of faking.

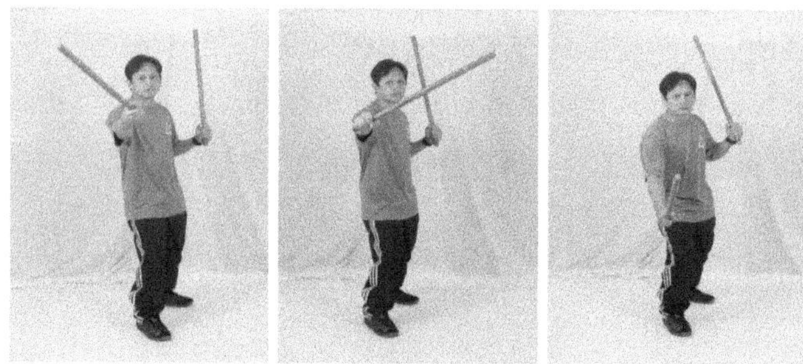

7. Exercise Drill: "Rapido Sonkete"

This exercise is a striking technique and is performed by alternating with each forward advancing foot work from the female triangle from right foot lead stance and the left foot lead stance. First, step forward into a right foot lead stance from a normal stance with your feet together at shoulder width apart. Grip each baston firmly near the "punyo" section of each baston with your elbows located near your right side and forearms parallel to the floor or ground, your bastons pointing upwards but not in a vertical position, only scantly pointing upwards. Now, begin this exercise or technique by simply bending both your elbows about 90 degrees, parallel to the floor or ground and extending your wrist upward as each baston extends upward delivering a "Sonkete" strike up to your opponent's lower left rib cage. Each "Sonkete" strike is executed in an alternating circular rapid motion of three (3) circular strikes per each baston. Execute this same exercise on the opposite side by simply alternating your right foot lead stance to a left foot lead stance from the female triangle, placing your weapons or bastons on your left side and deliver a "Sonkete" strike up to your opponent's lower right rib cage. Each "Sonkete" strike is executed in an alternating circular rapid motion of three (3) circular strikes per baston. Execute this ten (10) to fifteen (15) times depending on your speed and conditioning.

*Note: the above exercises or drills should take about fifteen (15) minutes to complete.

Chapter Six

Strikes

Formal Strikes

1. "Taga"

This strike is normally to an opponent's left temple in a right foot lead with a right-hand weapon inward strike at a 45-degree angle, but in a left foot lead stance this strike is called the **"San Miguel"**, striking with the right-hand weapon to an opponent's left temple and with the left-hand weapon the strike is to an opponent's right temple. Note: in the "Galleon Clan System" the **"Taga"** strike in a double weapon system is a diagonal strike from the open **"abierta"** position either right or left-handed.

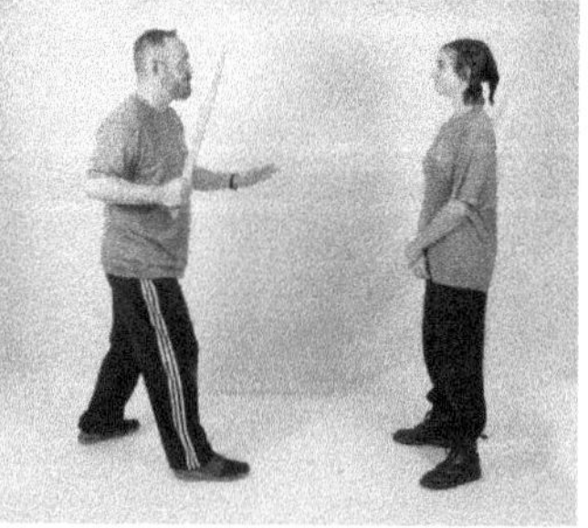

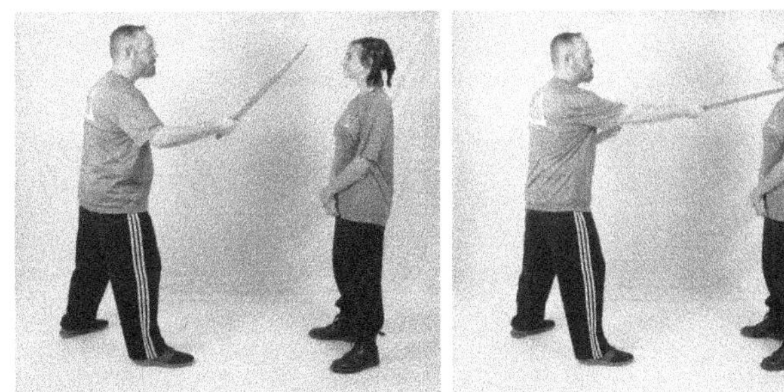

2. "Bartical"

This strike is normally to an opponent's right temple in a right foot lead with the right hand weapon backhand strike at 45-degree angle or with the left-hand weapon a backhand strike to an opponent's left temple in left foot lead stance. Note: in the "Galleon Clan System" the "Bartical" strike in a double weapon system is a diagonal strike from the closed, **"Cerrada,"** position either right or left-handed.

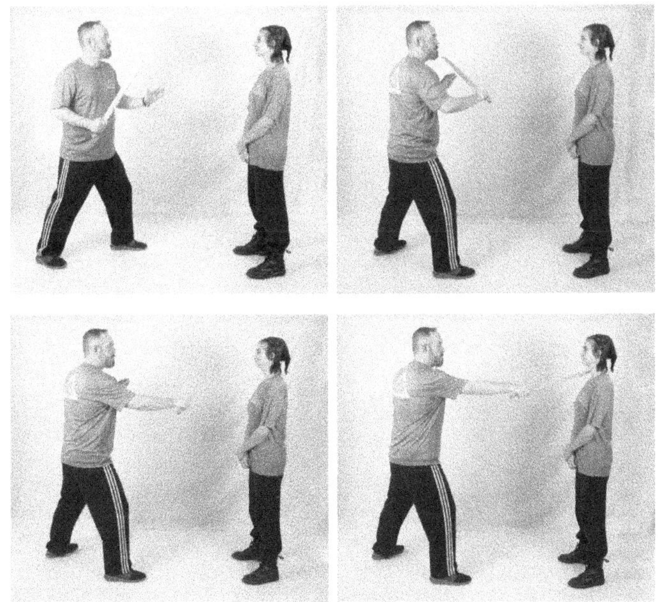

3. "Planchada-Abierta"

This strike is a horizontal inward strike to an opponent's left side midsection with the right-hand weapon in a right foot lead stance or with the left-hand weapon an inward strike to opponent's right-side midsection in a left foot lead stance.

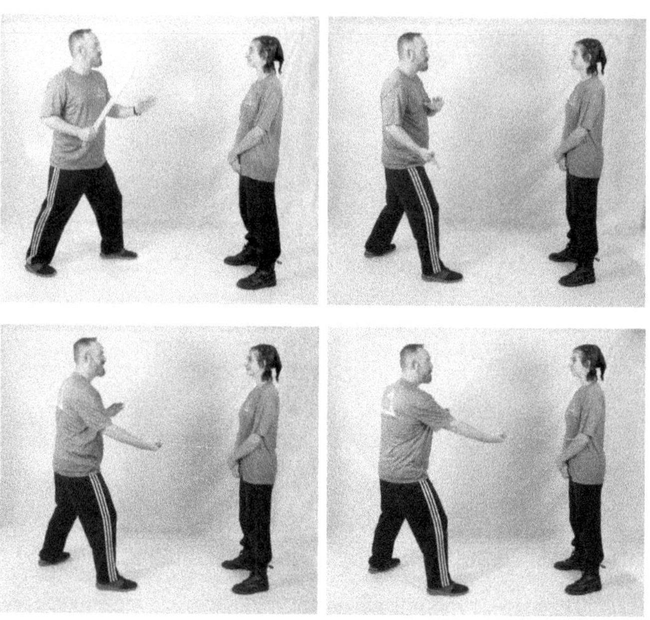

4. "Planchada-Cerrada"

This strike is a horizontal inward backhand strike to an opponent's right-side midsection with the right-hand weapon in a right foot lead stance or with the left-hand weapon an inward backhand strike to the opponent's left side midsection in a left foot lead stance.

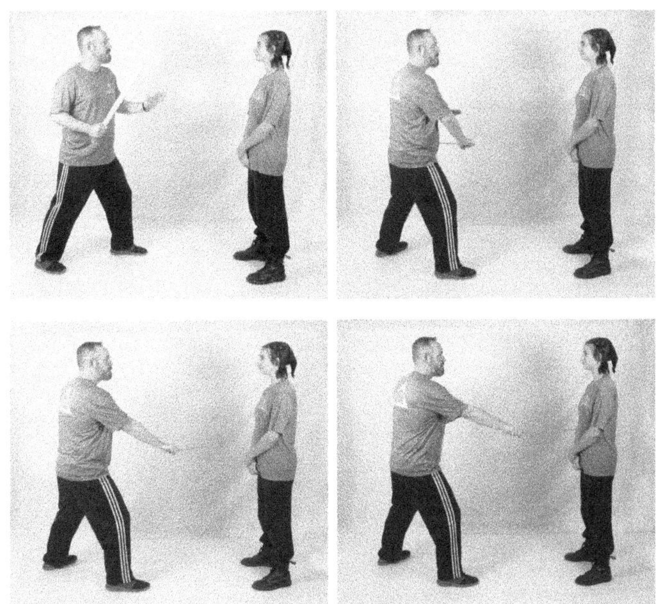

5. "Sak-Sak Lagusan"

This strike is a forward tunnel thrust strike to an opponent's midsection with the right-hand weapon in a right foot lead stance or with the left-hand weapon forward tunnel thrust strike to opponent's midsection in a left foot lead stance.

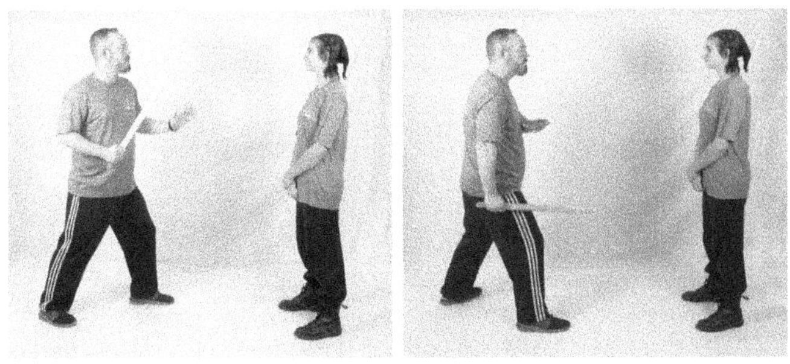

6. "Sak-Sak sa gawing Kanon" or "Clavada Afuera" or "Benediciones del Fraile"

This strike is a forward thrusting palm down strike to the opponent's left chest with the right-hand weapon in a right foot lead stance or with the left-hand weapon forward thrusting palm down strike to the opponent's right chest side in a left foot lead stance.

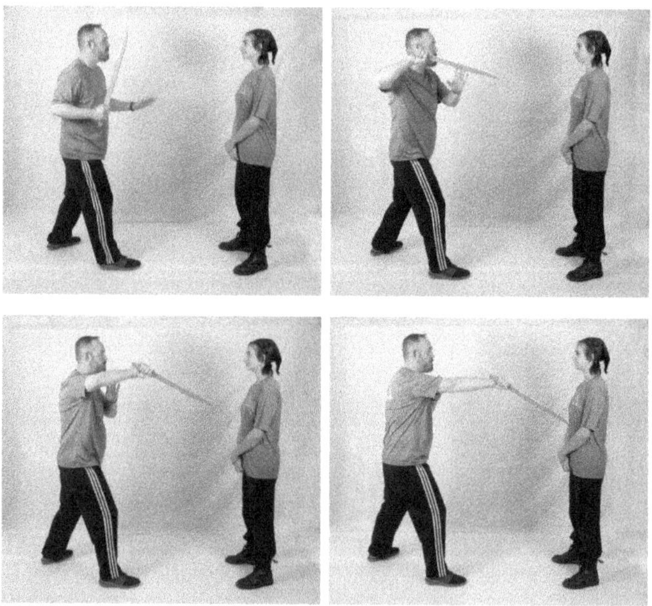

7. "Sak-Sak sa gawing Kaliwa" or "Clavada Adentro" or "Tusok Fraile"

This strike is a forward thrusting palm up strike to the opponent's right chest side with the right-hand weapon in a right foot lead stance or with the left-hand weapon a forward thrusting palm up strike to opponent's left chest side in a left foot lead stance.

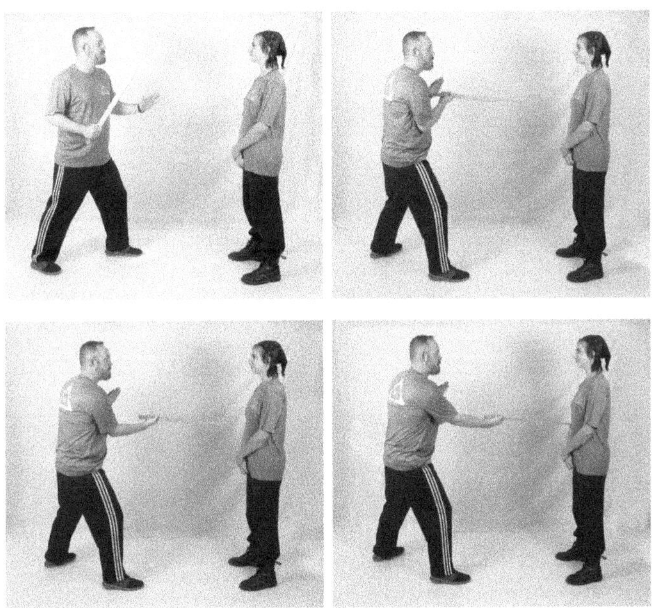

8. "Aldabis"

This strike is an upward, inward backhand strike starting from the lower left side and travels up across the body in a diagonal with the right-hand weapon in a right foot lead stance or with the left-hand weapon starting from the lower right side and travels up across the body in a diagonal with the left-hand weapon in a left foot lead stance. Note: in the "Galleon Clan system" the **"Aldabis"** strike in a double weapon system is a diagonal strike from the closed, **"Cerrada,"** position either right or left-handed.

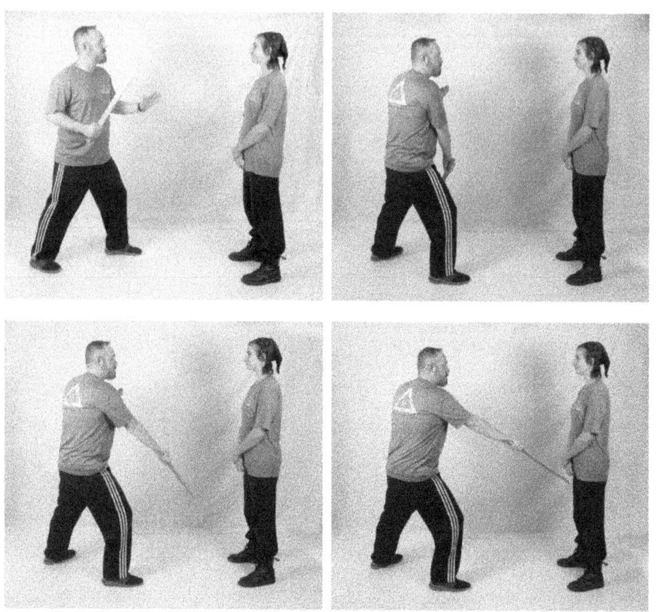

9. "Saboy"

This strike is an upward, inward, palm up forehand strike starting from the lower right side and travels up across the body in a diagonal with the right-hand weapon in a right foot lead stance or with the left-hand weapon starting from the lower left side and travels up across the body in a diagonal in a left foot lead stance. Note: in the "Galleon Clan System" the **"Saboy"** strike in a double weapon system is a diagonal strike from the open, **"Abierta,"** position either right or left-handed. In other systems, it is called or reference as "Aldabis".

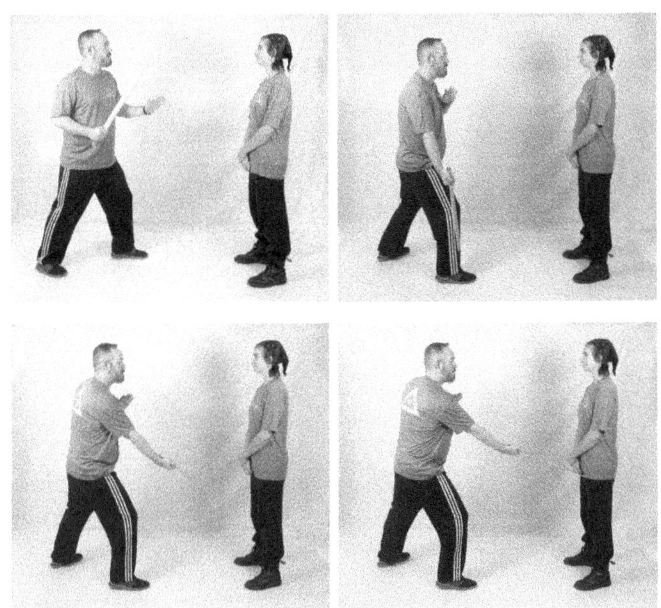

10. "Fraile Alto Afuera"

This strike is similar to the No.6 strike, but the target area is higher and to your opponent's left eye.

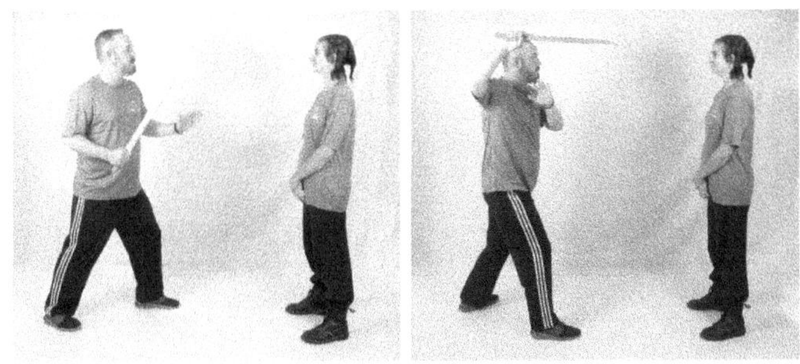

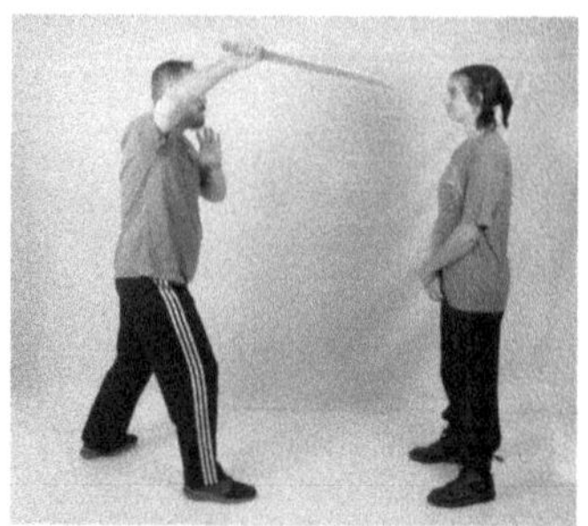 

11. "Fraile Alto Adentro"

This strike is similar to the No.7 strike, but the target area is higher and to your opponent's right eye.

12. "Tagang Buhat Araw" or "Tero Grave"

This strike is a vertical descending strike executed in a forward stance to the top of the head as the target area; it can cut through to the center line of the body, but the primary target is the opponent's head. It is also the No.12 strike in other "Visayan" Escrima systems. Sometimes, this technique can be reinforced with a "Redondo" before the strike to build up power during the delivery of this strike. This strike can also be reinforced with a **"Cola de Lagarto,"** which is a small circular wrist action used to build up power before delivery of any striking pattern. The practitioner may also incorporate the use of the **"Florette"** before a strike to build up power.

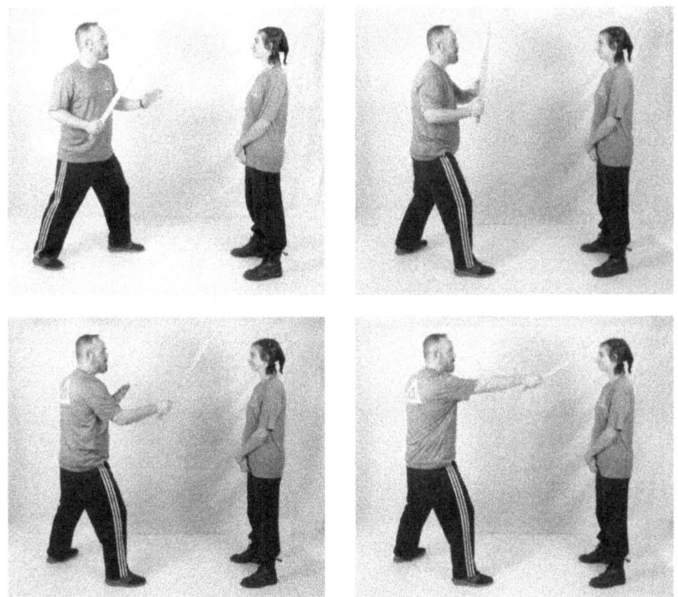

*Note: All the previous strikes can be adjusted to various targets areas, like **"Taga"** and **"Bartical"** strikes can be adjusted striking the temple, neck, or shoulder. The **"Planchada Abierta"** and **"Planchada Cerrada"** horizontal strikes can be delivered low line, middle line, or high line at any time depending on the situation, or window of opportunity, that might exist in real combat or sparring session.

Auxiliary Strikes

1. "Haklis"

This is a high scooping strike. The technique usually starts from the open/outside position, or No.1 **"Taga"** striking position, and arches downwards to upwards, towards the middle and upper part of the opponent's body. This strike is executed in the right foot forward stance but with the body elongated or extended out forward.

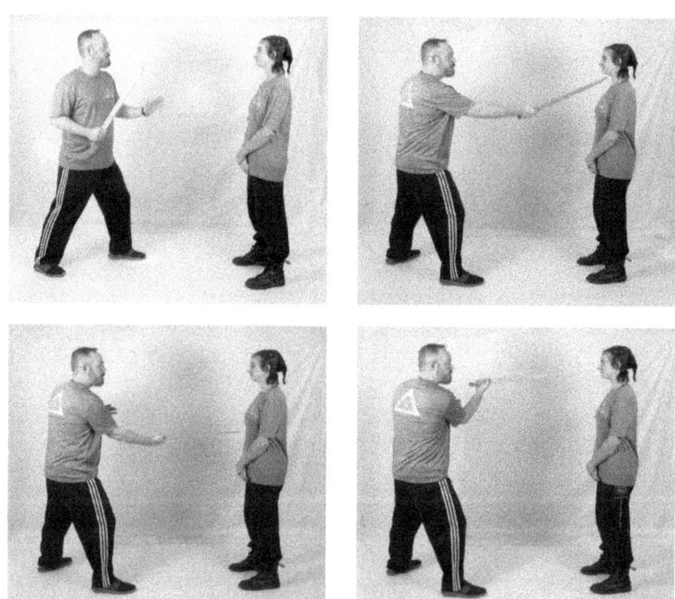

2. "Sablay"

This is a low scooping strike. The technique is like **"Haklis"** but has a lower target, and the primary target areas are the lower parts of the body between the knee and ankle. This technique usually starts from the open/outside position, or from the No.1 **"Taga"** striking position, and arches downwards to upwards, towards the knees or lower and upper part of the opponent's body. This strike is executed in the right foot forward stance but with the body elongated or extended out forward.

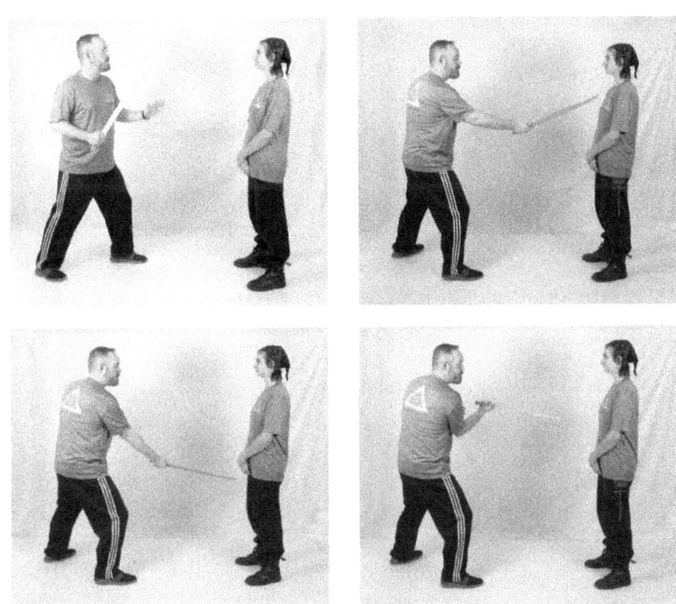

3. "Hulipas"

This is a high transition strike. The technique usually starts from the closed/inside position, or from the No.4 **"Planchada Cerrada"** striking position, and travels up and downwards diagonally across the opponent's body down through to the No.9 **"Saboy"** strike position. Note: this strike starts in the right foot lead stance and ends in the left foot lead stance.

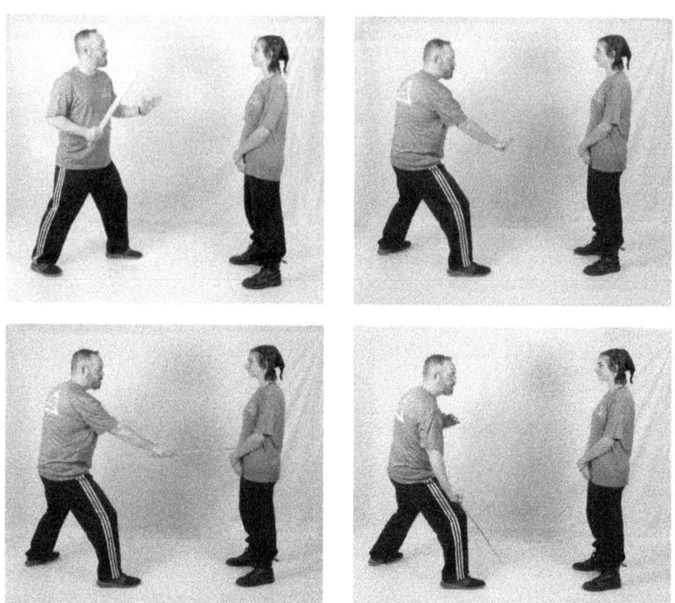

4. "Tigpas"

This is an inside, low diagonal and upward strike. The technique usually starts from the closed/inside position, or from the No.2 **"Bartical"** striking position, and travels downward diagonally across the opponent's body down through to the No.9 **"Saboy"** strike and then chambers up to the No.1 **"Taga"** strike position while keeping the cutting edge of the weapon facing the opponent. Note: this strike is executed in the right foot lead stance.

5. "Aldabis sa Itaas"

This is an inside, downward, steep diagonal strike, which is almost vertical. The technique usually starts from the open/outside position, or from the No.1 **"Taga"** striking position, and travels downward diagonally to the centerline of the opponent's body. Note this strike is executed in the right foot lead stance.

6. "Aldabis sa Ilalim"

This is an inside, upward, steep diagonal strike, which is almost vertical. The technique usually starts from the closed/inside position, or from the No.8 **"Aldabis"** striking position, and travels upwards, diagonally to the centerline of the opponent's body. Note: this strike is executed in the right foot lead stance and ends in left foot lead stance.

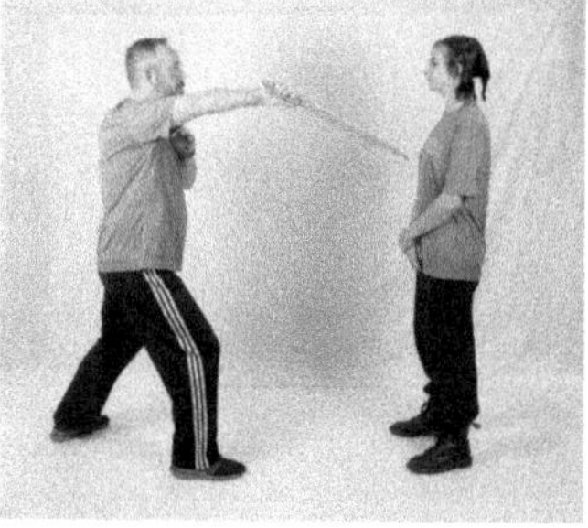

These are the 6 auxiliary strikes in the "Galleon Clan System of Escrima" and other Visayan tribal systems in the central regions of the Philippines Leyte, Cebu, and Boho.

CHAPTER SEVEN

Techniques

1. "Baguhan"/ "Novicio (a)"

This technique is based on inward high and inward low strikes. While in a left foot lead, **"Laban Handa"** stance or **"Mandirigma"** stance, with both of your weapons chambered at each side, pointing upwards in a vertical position ready to parry, defend or attack, step forward into a right foot lead stance. Note: this action of adjusting your foot work is called **"Columpio,"** which is a Chabacano and Spanish word that means "swing" as you adjust your feet rhythmically. As you are stepping into the right foot lead stance, you will be executing a high **"Planchada Abierta"** strike to your opponent's left shoulder with your right-hand weapon, but just before the high **"Planchada Abierta"** strike reaches its target, the target is now changed to the left temple of your opponent's head. This is accomplished by simply rotating the wrist of your right hand upward in a 45-degree angle, striking your opponent's left temple. Then, immediately rotate your weapon downward and strike your opponent's right knee with a back hand **"Aldabis"** strike. Immediately chamber your weapon back to your right side as you swing back into a left foot lead. Now, from the opposite side while in a left foot lead stance, with both of your weapons chambered at each side, pointing upwards in a vertical position ready to parry, defend or attack, step forward into a left foot lead stance. As you are stepping into the left foot lead stance, you will be executing a high **"Planchada Abierta"** strike to your opponent's right shoulder with your left-hand weapon, but just before the high **"Planchada Abierta"** strike reaches its target, the target is now changed to the right temple of your opponent's head. This is accomplished by simply rotating the wrist of your left hand upward in a 45-degree angle, striking your opponent's right temple. Then, immediately rotate your weapon downward and strike your opponent's right knee with a back hand **"Aldabis"** strike. Immediately chamber your weapon back as you back into a left foot lead **"Laban Handa"** stance or **"Mandirigma"** stance.

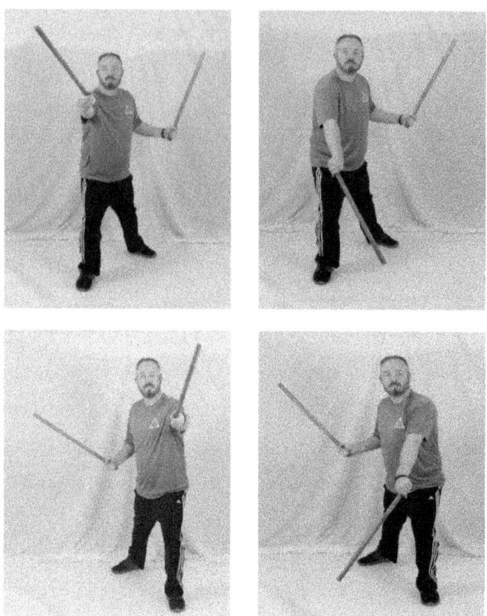

"Sombrada" or Partner Drill for "Baguhan" Inward, Back hand and Back Hand

This is a two-person basic Sinawali drill with both persons directly facing off each other while in a right foot lead stance. The Inward and Back Hand drill is basically an inward strike with the right-hand weapon to the opponent's left temple and immediately followed with a back hand strike with the same right-hand weapon to opponent's right knee. Immediately follow with an Inward **"Planchada"** strike, rotating the blade to strike with the right-hand weapon to your opponent's right neck. The Inward and Back Hand drill is divided up into three (3) target strike areas and is sometimes called High, Low or H, L. The high (H) target is your opponent's temple, the low (L) target is your opponent's knee and will consist with of following:

1. Right hand weapon target area is to your opponent's left temple and right knee.

2. Left hand weapon target area to your opponent's right temple and left knee.

Note: While executing this Inward High, Back Hand Low drill as you both target each target area, your weapons will hit each other forming an "X" at each height, High and Low. This drill or exercise can also be performed or executed in either a **"De Fondo"** planted right foot lead stance anchored to the ground or floor or executed using the female or male triangle foot work of continuously switching stances as you swing **"Columpio,"** your feet rhythmically from stance to stance and side to side.

2. "Abecedario"

This technique means Alphabet A, B, C's and is based on inward high, backhand low, and back hand high strikes. The technique is somewhat similar to the **"Baguhan."** While in a left foot lead, **"Laban Handa"** stance or **"Mandirigma"** stance, with both of your weapons chambered at each side pointing upwards in a vertical position ready to parry, defend or attack, step forward into a right foot lead stance. As you are stepping into the right foot lead stance, you will be executing a high **"Taga"** strike to your opponent's left temple. Then, immediately rotate your weapon downward and strike your opponent's right knee with a back hand **"Aldabis"** strike and chamber your right hand weapon up on your left side near your left shoulder while chambering your weapon up on your right side as if you were going to execute a **"Bartical"** backhand strike to your opponent's left temple, but instead rotate your wrist counter clockwise and execute a high **"Planchada Cerrada"** strike to your opponent's neck on the left side, chopping off your opponent's head. Note: this left wrist to an inward counterclockwise circular motion is also called **"Cola de Lagarto"** (the tail of the lizard), an aggressive, rapid whipping motion, strike. Next, step back into a left foot lead, **"Laban Handa"** stance or **"Mandirigma"** stance, with both of your weapons chambered at each side, your weapons pointing upwards in a vertical position. From this left foot lead stance, execute a "**Taga**" strike to your opponent's right temple. Then immediately rotate your weapon downward and strike your opponent's left knee with a back hand **"Aldabis"** strike. Chamber your left-hand weapon up on your right side near your right shoulder, and chamber your weapon up on your right side as if you were going to execute a **"Bartical"** backhand strike to your opponent's right temple, but instead rotate your wrist counter clockwise and execute a high **"Planchada Cerrada"** strike to your opponent's neck on the right side, chopping off your opponent's head. Next, step back into a right foot lead **"Laban Handa"** stance or **"Mandirigma"** stance with both of your weapons chambered at each side pointing upwards in a vertical position.

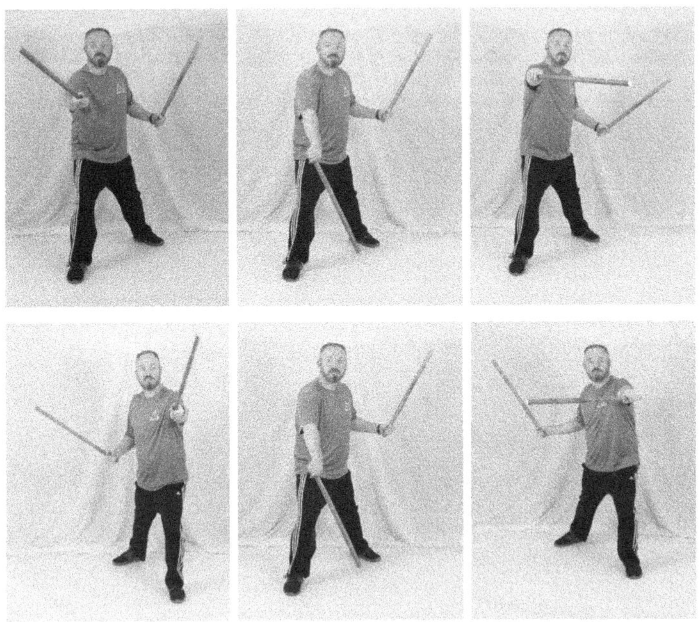

"Sombrada" or Partner Drill for "Abecedario" Inward High, Back Hand Low and Back Hand High

This is a two-person basic Sinawali drill with both persons directly facing off each other while in a Right Foot Lead Stance. This drill is sometimes called "**Abecedario**," or "A, B, C," and has a Filipino romantic expression for a three (3) strike combination. The Inward High, Back Hand Low and Back Hand High drill is basically an inward high strike with the right-hand weapon and immediately followed with a low back hand strike with the same right-hand weapon and immediately followed with a back hand high with the same right hand. This is immediately followed with an inward high strike with the left-hand weapon and immediately followed with a low back hand strike and a high back hand strike with the same left-hand weapon. The Inward High, Back Hand Low and Back Hand High drill is divided up into three (3) target strike areas and is sometimes called High, Low, High or H, L, H consisting of three (3) strikes per hand. High

Inward, Back Hand Low and Back Hand High will consist of the following:

1. The right-hand weapon executes three (3) strikes. Inward High target area is to your opponent's left temple and Back Hand Low target area is to your opponent's knee. A Back Hand High target area is to your opponent's right temple.

2. The left-hand weapon executes three (3) strikes. Inward High target area is to your opponent's right temple and Back Hand Low target area is to your opponent's knee. A Back Hand High target area is to your opponent's left temple.

Note: while executing this Inward High, Back Hand Low and Back Hand High drill as you both target each target area, your weapons will hit each other forming an "X" at each height High, Low and High. It is necessary to adjust your height or lower your stance and weapon for each target area. This drill sequence can be repeated several times depending on the instructor.

3. "Magbabayo"

This technique romantically refers to a "Downward Figure Eight Pattern Strike" and is an agricultural tool used in the Philippines to repair the earthen dikes on the hillsides that contains rice patties. It looks like a brick layer's trowel but smaller in size and is used in conjugation with a mortar like substance to repair the earthen dikes from leaking. The motion used in spreading the mortar like substance is a continuous interweaving downward figure eight pattern overlapping each other. This striking technique is based on this downward figure eight motion from this **"Magbabayo"** tool. Begin in a left foot lead, **"Laban Handa"** stance, or **"Mandirigma"** stance, with both of your weapons chambered at each side, pointing upwards in a vertical position ready to parry, defend or attack. Step forward into a right foot lead stance. As you are stepping into the right foot lead stance, execute with your right-hand weapon a downward figure eight striking pattern consisting of **"Taga"** and **"Bartical"** strikes. The **"Taga"** strike starts from the open, **"abierta,"** position from your right side and the target is to your opponent's left temple, neck, or shoulder. It is an inward, downward 45 degree angle slash that strikes through your intended target and goes down past your opponent's centerline to about your opponent's right hip and loops back up to the **"Bartical"** strike chambered closed, **"Cerrada,"** position on your left side. This continues with a downward 45 degree backhand slash to your opponent's right temple, neck or shoulder and strikes through your intended target, going down past your opponent's centerline to about your opponent's left hip, looping back up to the **"Taga"** start open, **"abierta,"** chambered position. Then immediately step forward into a left foot lead stance. As you are stepping into the left foot lead stance, execute with your left-hand weapon a downward figure eight striking pattern consisting of **"Taga"** and **"Bartical"** strikes. The **"Taga"** strike starts from the open, **"abierta,"** position from your left side and the target is to your opponent's right temple, neck or shoulder. It is an inward, downward 45 degree angle slash that strikes through your intended target and goes down past your opponent's centerline to about your opponent's left hip and loops back up to the **"Bartical"** strike chambered closed, **"Cerrada,"** position on your right side. This continues with a downward 45 degree backhand slash to your opponent's left temple, neck or shoulder and strikes through your intended target, going down past your opponent's centerline to about your opponent's right hip, looping back up to the **"Taga"** start open, **"Abierta,"** chambered position.

"Sombrada" or Partner Drill for "Magbabayo" Downward Inward and Back Hand

This is a two-person basic Sinawali drill with both persons directly facing off each other while in a right foot lead stance. The **"Magbabayo"** drill is basically an inward strike with the right-hand weapon and travels down and up to the "Bartical" position. It is immediately followed with a back hand strike with the same right-hand weapon, down to the "Saboy" position, looping back up to the **"Taga"** position, forming a flat lazy figure eight. Immediately execute an inward strike with the left-hand weapon and travel down and up to the **"Bartical"** position. Follow with a back hand strike with the same left-hand weapon, down to the **"Saboy"** position, looping back up to the **"Taga"** position, forming a flat lazy figure eight. The **"Magbabayo"** consists of a High (H) line target area to your opponent's left temple and right temple. This will consist of the following:

1. Right hand weapon target area is to your opponent's left temple and right temple and is executed with two (2) strikes Inward high line to left temple and Back Hand high line to right temple.

2. Left hand weapon target area is to your opponent's right temple and left temple is executed with two (2) strikes Inward high line to right temple and Back Hand high line to left temple.

Note: while executing this "**Magbabayo**" drill as you both target each target area; your weapons will hit each other forming an "X" at each centerline. This drill or exercise can also be performed or executed in either a **"De Fondo"** planted right foot lead stance anchored to the ground or floor or executed using the female triangle foot work of continuously switching stances as you swing **"Columpio"** your feet rhythmically from stance to stance and side to side.

4. "Magbabayo Invertido"

This technique romantically refers to an "Upward Figure Eight Pattern Strike". While in a left foot lead, **"Laban Handa"** stance or **"Mandirigma"** stance, with both of your weapons chambered at each side pointing upwards in a vertical position ready to parry, defend or attack, step forward into a right foot lead stance. As you are stepping into the right foot lead stance, execute with your right-hand weapon an upward figure eight striking pattern consisting of **"Saboy"** and **"Aldabis"** strikes. The **"Saboy"** strike starts from the open, **"Abierta,"** position from your right side and the target is to your opponent's left hip, thigh, or left knee. It is an inward, upward 45 degree angle diagonal slash that strikes through your intended target and goes up past your opponent's centerline to about your opponent's right shoulder, looping back down to the **"Aldabis"** strike chambered closed, **"Cerrada,"** position on your left side. This continues with an upward 45 degree backhand diagonal slash to your opponent's right hip, thigh or knee, striking through your intended target and goes up pass your opponent's centerline to about your opponent's left shoulder, looping back down to the **"Saboy"** start open **"Abierta"** chambered position. Immediately step forward into a left foot lead stance. As you are stepping into the left foot lead stance, execute with your left-hand weapon a downward figure eight striking pattern consisting of **"Saboy"** and **"Aldabis"** strikes. The **"Saboy"** strike starts from the open, **"Abierta,"** position from your left side and the target is to your opponent's right hip, thigh, or knee. It is an inward, upward 45 degree angle diagonal slash, striking through your intended target and goes up past your opponent's centerline to about your opponent's left shoulder, looping back down to the **"Aldabis"** strike chambered closed, **"Cerrada,"** position on your right side. Continue with a upward 45 degree diagonal backhand slash to your opponent's left hip, thigh or knee, striking through your intended target and going up past your opponent's centerline to about your opponent's right shoulder, looping back down to the **"Saboy"** start open, **"Abierta,"** chambered position.

"Sombrada" or Partner Drill for "Magbabayo Invertido" Upward Figure Eight

This is a two-person basic Sinawali drill with both persons directly facing each other while in a Right Foot Lead Stance. The "**Magbabayo Invertido**" drill is an inward upward diagonal strike with the right-hand weapon, traveling up from the "**Saboy**" position and down to the "**Aldabis**" position. This is immediately followed with a back hand strike with the same right-hand weapon up to the "**Taga**" position, looping back down to the "**Saboy**" position, forming a flat, lazy figure eight. Immediately execute an inward upward diagonal strike with the left-hand weapon, traveling up to the "**Bartical**" position, looping down to the "**Aldabis**" position. Immediately follow with a back hand "**Aldabis**" strike with the same left-hand weapon up to the "**Taga**" position, looping back down to the "**Saboy**" position forming a flat, lazy figure eight. The "**Magbabayo Invertido**" consists of a low line target area to your opponent's left knee and right knee. This will consist of the following:

1. Right hand weapon target area is to your opponent's left knee and right knee and is executed with two (2) strikes Inward low line to left knee and Back Hand low line to right knee.

2. Left hand weapon target area is to your opponent's right knee and left knee and is executed with two (2) strikes Inward low line to right knee and Back Hand low line to left knee.

Note: while executing this **"Magbabayo Invertido"** drill, you both target each target area; your weapons will hit each other forming an "X" at each centerline. This drill or exercise can also be performed or executed in either a **"De Fondo"** planted right foot lead stance anchored to the ground or floor or executed using the female triangle foot work of continuously switching stances as you swing **"Columpio"** your feet rhythmically from stance to stance and side to side.

5. **"Kaluban"**

This technique refers to "Drawing of the Sword(s) and means to pull your sword(s) out ready for combat from a case called a "sheath," which is usually tied or attached to your left side. The sword is pulled out with your right hand either to quickly deliver a strike or to begin a combat confrontation. But in **"Lakbay Sinawali,"** it has reference to a double diagonal cut from a "Crusada Cerrada," crossed closed position, and drawing the double swords out to an **"Abierta,"** open position, with one sword cutting up diagonally and the other sword cutting down diagonally in the opposite direction of each other at the same time. This shearing technique of drawing the swords can also be executed with both swords crossed on a level **"Planchada"** plane, like shearing off your opponent's head. Begin in a left foot lead, **"Laban Handa"** stance or **"Mandirigma"** stance, with both of your weapons chambered at each side, pointing upwards in a vertical position ready to parry, defend or attack. Step forward into a right foot lead stance. As you are stepping into the right foot lead stance, execute with your right-hand weapon a downward 45-degree diagonal **"Taga"** strike across your opponent's torso. At the same time, with your left-hand weapon, you will execute an upward 45-degree diagonal **"Saboy"** strike across your opponent's torso. Note: The right-hand weapon should be on top of your left-hand weapon as you execute double diagonal slashes. Once both inward diagonal slashes are completed, hands should be crossed at the center line of your opponent's mid-section. Next, immediately rotate your right-hand weapon counterclockwise and your left-hand weapon clockwise. With this rotating action, your cutting edges of your swords will be positioned for the diagonal shearing action as you draw the swords simultaneously out to the **"Abierta,"** open position, while executing a double shearing cut against your opponent's torso. As the action of the shearing and drawing of the swords is being executed, you should adjust and swing your right foot back so that you will now be in a left foot lead, **"Laban Handa"** stance or **"Mandirigma"** stance. Now, you are in a left foot lead stance. As you are in the left foot lead stance, execute with your left-hand weapon a downward 45-degree diagonal **"Taga"** strike across your opponent's torso and at the same time, with your right-hand weapon, execute an upward 45-degree diagonal **"Saboy"** strike across your opponent's torso. Note: The left-hand weapon should be on top of your right-hand weapon as you execute these double diagonal slashes. Once both inward diagonal slashes are completed, both hands should be crossed at the center line of your opponent's mid-section. Then immediately rotate your left-hand weapon clockwise and your right-hand weapon counterclockwise. With this rotating action, your cutting edges of your swords will be positioned for the diagonal shearing action as you draw the swords simultaneously out to the **"Abierta,"** open position, while executing a double shearing cut against your opponent's torso. As the action of the shearing and drawing of the swords is being executed, you should adjust and swing your left foot back so that you will now be in a right foot lead, **"Laban Handa"** stance or **"Mandirigma"** stance.

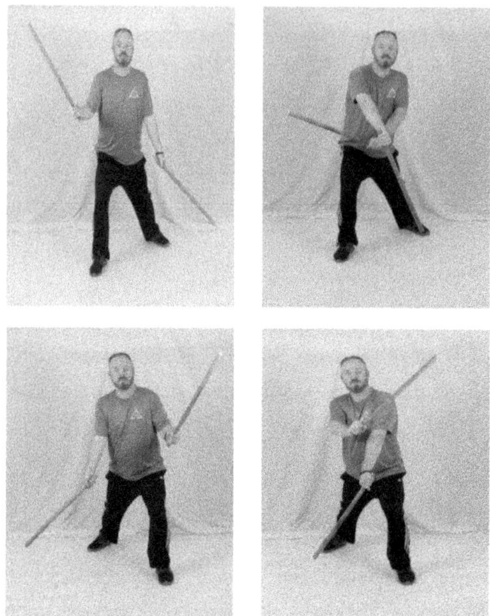

"Sombrada" or Partner Drill for "Kaluban"

This is a two-person basic Sinawali drill with both persons directly facing off while in a Left Foot Lead **"Laban Handa"** stance or **"Mandirigma"** stance. Note: this drill is difficult to have both you and your training partner striking each other's weapons. For this drill, it is best to position yourselves into a "Largo Mano" distance so that your weapons will not touch or strike each other. Just step into each striking position in mirror of each other and step out backwards. Visualize cutting your opponent's torso diagonally as you execute the double sword shearing action.

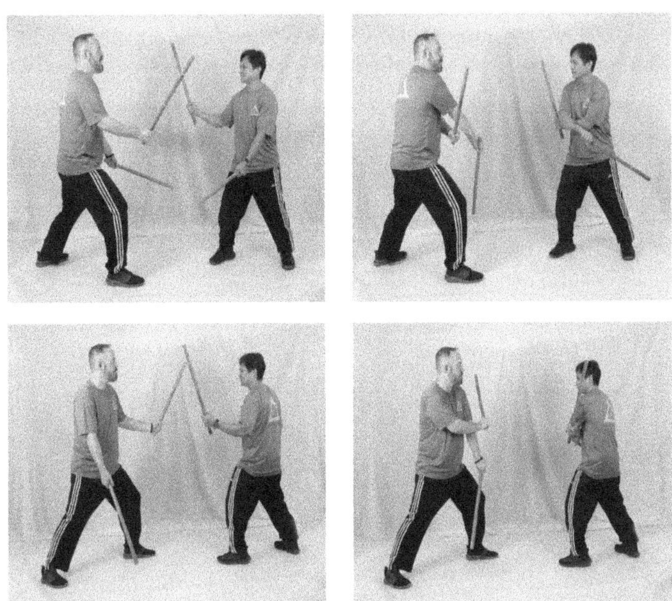

6. "Cinco Tero"

This technique refers to a five (5) angle striking pattern. Note: with a double weapon system, this technique is very similar to the **"Kaluban"** drawing of the swords. Begin in a left foot lead, **"Laban Handa"** stance or **"Mandirigma"** stance, with both of your weapons chambered at each side pointing upwards in a vertical position ready to parry, defend, or attack. Step forward into a right foot lead stance. As you are stepping into the right foot lead stance, execute with your right-hand weapon a downward 45-degree diagonal **"Taga"** strike across your opponent's torso. At the same time, with you left hand weapon, execute an upward 45-degree diagonal **"Saboy"** strike across your opponent's torso. Note: the right-hand weapon should be on top of your left-hand weapon as you execute these double diagonal slashes. Once both inward diagonal slashes are completed, your hands should be crossed at the center line of your opponent's mid-section. Immediately, rotate your right-hand weapon counterclockwise and your left-hand weapon clockwise. With this rotating action, your cutting edges of your swords will be positioned for the diagonal shearing action as you draw the swords simultaneously out to the **"Abierta,"** open, position while executing a double shearing cut against your opponent's torso. As the action of the shearing and drawing of the swords is being executed, you should step forward into a left foot lead stance. As you are in the left foot lead stance, execute with your left-hand weapon a downward 45-degree diagonal **"Taga"** strike across your opponent's torso. At the same time with your right-hand weapon, execute an upward 45-degree diagonal **"Saboy"** strike across your opponent's torso. Note: the left-hand weapon should be on top of your right-hand weapon as you execute this double diagonal slashes. Once both inward diagonal slashes are completed, both hands should be crossed at the center line of your opponent's mid-section. Then, immediately rotate your left-hand weapon clockwise and your right-hand weapon counterclockwise. With this rotating action, your cutting edges of your swords will be positioned for the diagonal shearing action. As you draw the swords simultaneously out to the **"Abierta,"** open, position execute a double shearing cut against your opponent's torso. As the action of the shearing and drawing of the swords is executed, immediately step forward with your right foot into a right foot lead stance. As you are stepping into the right foot lead stance, execute double over, under twin **"Sak-Sak"** strike called **"Avalanche Doble."** With your right-hand weapon, execute a tunnel trust to your opponent's mid-section at center line. With your left-hand weapon elevated directly overhead, execute a tunnel trust at your opponent's face or neck at center line. Note: the **"Avalanche Doble"** should be executed at the same time. Next, pull your weapons out by simply turning them ¼ turn counterclockwise. Then, rotate your left-hand weapon down counter-clockwise and right-hand weapon counter-clockwise up. So, that your two swords will be in the "Crusada Cerrada," 45-degree diagonal, with the right-hand weapon on top pointing downward and left-hand weapon on the bottom pointing upward. Now the edges of your swords will be positioned for the diagonal shearing action as you draw the swords simultaneously out to the **"Abierta,"** open, position while executing a double shearing cut against your opponent's torso. As the action of the shearing and drawing of the swords is executed, immediately step backwards with your right foot into a left foot lead, **"Laban Handa"** stance or **"Mandirigma"** stance. Since you are already in a left foot lead stance, lean forward with 60% of your weight on your forward left foot and 40% of your weight is on your rear right foot extended out, straight, and adjusted to directly behind your right foot. Note: this action of rhythmically adjusting your foot work is called **"Columpio,"** which is a Chabacano or Spanish word that means "swing." From this left foot lead stance, execute with your left-hand weapon a downward 45-degree diagonal **"Taga"** strike across your opponent's torso. At the same time with you right hand weapon, execute an upward 45-degree diagonal **"Saboy"** strike across your opponent's torso. Note: the left-hand weapon should be on top of your right-hand weapon as you execute these double diagonal slashes. Once both inward diagonal slashes are completed, hands should be crossed at the center line of your opponent's mid-section. Then, immediately rotate your left-hand weapon clockwise and your right-hand weapon counterclockwise. With this rotating action, your cutting edges of your swords will be positioned for the diagonal shearing action as you draw the swords simultaneously out to the **"Abierta,"** open, position while executing a double shearing cut against your opponent's torso. As the action of the shearing and drawing of the swords is being executed, you should step forward into a right lead stance with 60% of your weight on your forward right foot and 40% of your weight is on your rear left foot extended out, straight, and adjusted to directly behind your right foot. As you are in the right foot lead stance, execute with your right-hand weapon a downward 45-degree diagonal **"Taga"** strike across your opponent's torso. At the same time with your left-hand weapon, execute an upward 45-degree diagonal **"Saboy"** strike across your opponent's torso. Note: the right-hand weapon should be on top of your left-hand weapon as you execute these double diagonal slashes. Once both inward diagonal slashes are completed, both hands should be crossed at the center line of your opponent's mid-section. Immediately rotate your right-hand weapon counterclockwise and your left-hand weapon clockwise. With this rotating action your cutting edges of your swords will be positioned for the diagonal shearing action as you draw the swords simultaneously out to the **"Abierta,"** open, position while executing a double shearing cut against your opponent's torso. As the action of the shearing and drawing of the swords is executed, immediately step forward with your left foot into a left foot lead stance. As you are stepping into the left foot lead stance, execute double over, under twin **"Sak-Sak"** strike called **"Avalanche Doble"** with your left-hand weapon executing a tunnel thrust to your opponent's mid-section at center line. Your right-hand weapon is elevated directly overhead, executing a tunnel thrust at your opponent's face or neck at center line. Note: the **"Avalanche Doble"** should be executed at the same time. Next pull your weapons out by simply turning them ¼ turn clockwise. Then rotate your right-hand weapon down clockwise and left-hand weapon clockwise, up. As a result, your two swords will be in the "Crusada Cerrada" 45-degree diagonal with the left-hand weapon on top pointing downward and right-hand weapon on the bottom pointing upward. Now, with the edges of your swords will be positioned for the diagonal shearing action as you draw the swords simultaneously out to the **"Abierta,"** open, position while executing a double shearing cut against your opponent's torso. As the action of the shearing and drawing of the swords is executed, immediately step backwards with your left foot into a right foot lead, **"Laban Handa"** stance or **"Mandirigma"** stance.

"Sombrada" or partner Drill for Cinco Tero"

This is a two-person basic Sinawali drill with both persons directly facing off while in a left foot lead **"Laban Handa"** stance or **"Mandirigma"** stance. This is very similar to the **"Kaluban"** Drill but is a continuous advancing drill until you draw the swords out back after the **"Avalanche Doble"** is pulled out.

Note: this drill is difficult to have both you and your training partner striking each other's weapons. For this drill it is best to position yourselves into a "Largo Mano" distance so that your weapons will not touch or strike each other. Just step into each striking position, mirroring each other and step out backwards. Visualize cutting your opponent's torso diagonally as you execute the double sword shearing action.

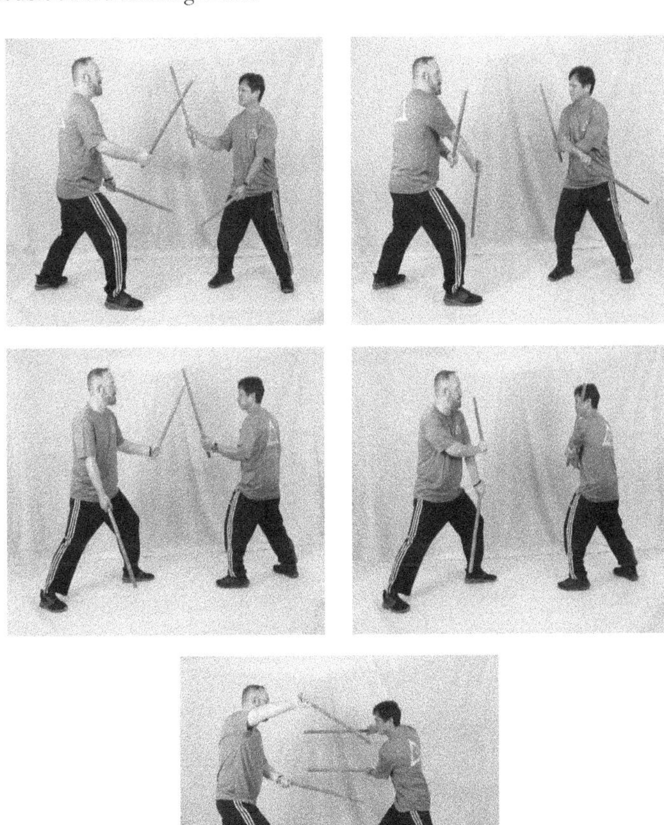

7. "Cielo Seis" or "Langit"

This technique means "Heaven" in Tagalog and is based on the principle of Inward High, Back Hand High and Back Hand High. This technique has a Filipino romantic expression for three (3) high line striking weaving combinations right and left. While in a left foot lead, **"Laban Handa"** stance or **"Mandirigma"** stance, with both of your weapons chambered at each side pointing upwards in a vertical position ready to parry, defend, or attack, step forward into a right foot lead stance and swing **"Columpio"** your left foot to directly behind your right foot lead stance. Execute the Inward high strike starting with the right-hand weapon. The target is to your opponent's left temple, neck, or shoulder, as you are executing this inward high line strike. Stepping forward with your right foot, chamber your left-hand weapon under your right armpit with the cutting edge of your sword facing your opponent. Note: this action of stepping forward and chambering your left-hand weapon under your right armpit is in reality a parry, block or strike. The reason you do not simply chamber your left-hand weapon under your right armpit is because it will completely expose your left side for a counter strike. You simply step into the chamber after a left-hand weapon parry, block, or strike as you execute the first inward high line strike with your right-hand weapon. Then immediately follow with a back hand high strike with the left-hand weapon that is chambered under the right arm pit. It is the same target area of the first strike and immediately followed with a back hand high strike with the right-hand weapon, which is now chambered on your left side, near your left shoulder. The target area of this right back hand strike is to your opponent's right temple, neck, or shoulder. Once the first three (3) series of strikes are completed from the right foot lead stance, you are chambering your right-hand weapon under your left armpit. You will now swing **"Columpio"** your right foot back and step forward with your left foot into a left foot lead stance. Now you are in a left foot lead stance, 60% of your weight is on your forward left foot and 40% of your weight is on your rear right foot extended out, straight. Next, swing **"Columpio,"** your left foot to be adjusted directly behind your right foot lead stance. Execute the inward high strike starting with the left-hand weapon. The target is to your opponent's right temple, neck, or shoulder as you are executing this inward high line strike. Stepping forward with your right foot, chamber your right-hand weapon under your left armpit with the cutting edge of your sword facing your opponent. Immediately follow with a back hand high strike with the right-hand weapon that is chambered under the left arm pit with the same target area of the first strike. This is immediately followed with a back hand high strike with the left-hand weapon, which is now chambered on your right side, near your right shoulder. The target area of this left back hand strike is to your opponent's left temple, neck, or left shoulder. Once the second three (3) series of strikes are completed from the left foot lead stance, you are chambering your left-hand weapon under your right armpit. You will now swing, **"Columpio,"** your left foot back and step forward with your right foot into a right foot lead stance with 60% of your weight on your forward left foot lead stance, and 40% of your weight on your rear left foot extended out, straight, and directly behind your right foot while completing the Heaven Six strike series. The Heaven Six Inward High, Back Hand High and Back Hand High is divided up into three (3) target strike areas and is sometimes called High, High, High or H, H, H consisting of three (3) strikes per side.

"Sombrada" or partner Drill for "Cielo Seis" Heaven Drill

1. The Right-Hand weapon executes a three (3) strike combination. Starting from the right side with the right-hand weapon, execute an Inward High target to your opponent's left temple. With your left-hand weapon, which is chambered under your right arm pit, execute a left-hand Back Hand High target to your opponent's left temple. Now chambered on your left side in the No. 2 "**Bartical**" strike position from after the first right hand strike, execute a high right-hand back hand strike targeting your opponent's right temple.

2. The left-hand weapon executes a three (3) strike combination. Starting from the left side with the left-hand weapon, execute a high inward strike targeting your opponent's right temple. With your right-hand weapon, which is chambered under your left arm pit, execute a high right back hand strike targeting your opponent's right temple. Now chambered on your right side in the No. 2 "**Bartical**" strike position from after the first left hand strike, execute a high left back hand strike targeting your opponent's left temple.

Note: Execute this Inward High, Back Hand High and Back Hand High drill as you both target one another's target area; your weapons will hit each other forming an "X" at each High, High and High. It is necessary to adjust your height or lower your stance and weapon for each target area. This drill sequence can be repeated several times depending on the instructor and can be performed in a stationary manner in a "De Fondo" stance or in a "**Luton**" flowing foot work. As you change into either a right foot lead or into a left foot lead stance, adjust your rear leg and foot in a "**Columpio**" manner.

8. "Cielo y Tierra Seis" or "Langit at Lupa"

This technique means **"Heaven and Earth"** in Tagalog and is based on the principle of Inward High, Back Hand Low and Back Hand High. This technique has a Filipino romantic expression for three (3) right and left striking and weaving combinations consisting of High, Low, High. In some systems it is also called **"Standard Six"**. While in a left foot lead, **"Laban Handa"** stance or **"Mandirigma"** stance, with both of your weapons chambered at each side pointing upwards in a vertical position ready to parry, defend or attack, step forward into a right foot lead stance and execute the Inward high strike, starting with the right-hand weapon targeting your opponent's left temple, neck, or shoulder. As you are executing this inward high line strike and stepping forward with your right foot, chamber your left-hand weapon under your right armpit with the cutting edge of your sword facing your opponent. Note: this action of stepping forward and chambering your left-hand weapon under your right armpit is in reality a parry, block, or strike. The reason is you do not simply chamber your left-hand weapon under your right armpit is it will completely expose your left side for a counter strike. You simply step into the chamber after a left-hand weapon parry, block, or strike as you execute the first inward high line strike with your right-hand weapon. Then, immediately follow with a back hand low strike with the left-hand weapon that is chambered under the right arm pit to the target area to your opponent's left knee. Immediately follow with a back hand high strike with the right-hand weapon, which is now chambered on your left side, near your left shoulder. The target area of this right back hand strike is to your opponent's right temple, neck, or shoulder. Once the first three (3) series of strikes are completed from the right foot lead stance, chamber your right-hand weapon under your left armpit. You will now swing **"Columpio"** your right foot back and step forward with your left foot into a left foot lead stance. Now, execute the Inward high strike starting with the left-hand weapon targeting your opponent's right temple, neck, or shoulder. As you are executing this inward high line strike, step forward with your right foot, chamber your right-hand weapon under your left armpit with the cutting edge of your sword facing your opponent. Then immediately follow with a back hand low strike with the right-hand weapon that is chambered under the left arm pit to the target area of your opponent's right knee. Immediately follow with a back hand high strike with the left-hand weapon, which is now chambered on your right side near your right shoulder. The target area of this left back hand strike is to your opponent's left temple, neck, or shoulder. Once the second third (3) series of strikes are completed from the left foot lead stance, chamber your left-hand weapon under your right armpit. You will now swing **"Columpio"** your left foot back and step forward with your right foot into a right foot lead stance completing the Heaven and Earth Six strike series.

The Heaven and Earth Six Inward High, Back Hand Low and Back Hand High is divided up into three (3) target strike areas and is sometimes called High, Low, High or (H, L, H) consisting of three (3) strikes per side.

"Sombrada" or Partner Drill for "Cielo y Tierra Seis" Heaven and Earth

1. The right-hand weapon executes a three (3) strike combination. Starting from the right side with the right-hand weapon, execute an Inward High strike targeting your opponent's left temple. With your left-hand weapon, which is chambered under your right arm pit, execute a left-hand Back Hand Low strike targeting your opponent's left knee. Now, chambered on your left side in the No. 2 "**Bartical**" strike position from after the first right hand strike, execute a right-hand Back Hand High target to your opponent's right temple.

2. The left-hand weapon executes a three (3) strike combination. Starting from the left side with the left-hand weapon, execute an Inward High strike

targeting your opponent's right temple. With your right-hand weapon, which is chambered under your left arm pit, execute a right Back Hand Low strike targeting your opponent's right knee. Now chambered on your right side in the No. 2 "**Bartical**" strike position from after the first left hand strike, execute a left Back Hand High strike targeting your opponent's left temple.

Note: While executing this Inward High, Back Hand Low and Back Hand High drill as you both target one another's target area, your weapons will hit each other forming an "X" at each height High, Low and High. It is necessary to adjust your height or lower your stance and weapon for each target area. This drill sequence can be repeated several times, depending on the instructor, and can be performed in a stationary manner using a "**De Fondo**" stance or in a "**Luton**" flowing foot work. As you change into either a right foot lead or a left foot lead stance, adjust your rear leg and foot in a "**Columpio**" manner.

9. "Salot Saboy"

This technique is an upward six strike combination and has a meaning of shoulder and hip respectively, but the true meaning or the romantic Filipino reference as applied to Escrima is **"Scoop and Throw."** Just picture yourself scooping in a bag of rice seeds hanging at your hips and grabbing the seeds in your hand, launching the seeds into the air. This technique is based on the principle of Inward Low, Back Hand Low and Back Hand Low. This technique of three (3) weaving combinations right and left consists of Low, Low, Low all traveling upwards in a diagonal direction, consisting of **"Saboy," "Aldabis," "Aldabis"** striking combinations on each side. While in a left foot lead, **"Laban Handa"** stance or **"Mandirigma"** stance, with both of your weapons chambered at each side pointing upwards in a vertical position ready to parry, defend, or attack, step forward into a right foot lead stance and execute the Inward low **"Saboy"** strike starting with the right-hand weapon targeting your opponent's left knee. As you are executing this inward low line strike and stepping forward with your right foot, chamber your left-hand weapon over on top of your right forearm with the cutting edge of your sword facing your opponent. Note: this action of stepping forward and chambering your left-hand weapon on top of your right forearm is in reality a parry, block, or strike. Again, you do not simply chamber your left-hand weapon on top your right forearm because it will completely expose your left side for a counter strike. You simply step into the chamber after a left-hand weapon parry, block, or strike. As you execute the first inward low line **"Saboy"** strike with your right-hand weapon to your opponent's left knee, immediately follow with a back hand low **"Aldabis"** strike with the left-hand weapon that is chambered on top of the right forearm to your opponent's left knee. Follow immediately with a back hand low "**Aldabis**" strike with the right-hand weapon to your opponent's right knee. The first three (3) series of strikes are completed from the right foot lead stance as you are chambering your right-hand weapon on top of your left forearm. You will now swing **"Columpio"** your right foot back and step forward with your left foot into a left foot lead stance with 60% of your weight on your forward left foot lead stance. Now, execute the Inward low **"Saboy"** strike starting with the left-hand weapon, targeting your opponent's right knee. As you are executing this inward low line **"Saboy"** strike and stepping forward with your left foot, chamber your right-hand weapon on top of your left forearm with the cutting edge of your sword facing your opponent. Note: This action of stepping forward and chambering your right-hand weapon on top of your left forearm is in reality a parry, block or strike. Again, you do not simply chamber your right-hand weapon on top your left forearm because it will completely expose your right side for a counter strike. You simply step into the chamber after a right-hand weapon parry, block, or strike as you execute the first inward low line **"Saboy"** strike with your left-hand weapon to your opponent's right knee. Immediately follow with a back hand low **"Aldabis"** strike with the right-hand weapon that is chambered on top of the left forearm to your opponent's right knee and follow with a back hand low "**Aldabis**" strike with the left-hand weapon to your opponent's left knee. Once the second third (3ʳᵈ) series of **"Saboy"**, **"Aldabis"**, **"Aldabis"** strikes are completed from the left foot lead stance, chamber your left-hand weapon on top of your right forearm. You will now swing, **"Columpio,"** your left foot back and step forward with your right foot into a right foot lead stance completing the **"Salot Saboy"** Six strike series. The "**Salot Saboy**" Six Inward Low, Back Hand Low and Back Hand Low is divided up into three (3) target strike areas and is sometimes called Low, Low, Low or (L, L, L) consisting of three (3) strikes per side of **"Saboy"**, **"Aldabis"**, **"Aldabis"**.

"Sombrada" or Partner Drill for "Salot Saboy"

1. The right-hand weapon executes a three (3) strike combination. Starting from the right side with the right-hand weapon, execute an Inward Low target to your opponent's left knee. With your left-hand weapon, which is chambered on top of your right forearm, execute a left-hand Back Hand Low target to your opponent's left knee. Now chambered on your left side in the "**Aldabis**" strike position from after the first right hand strike, execute a right-hand Back Hand Low target to your opponent's right knee.

2. The left-hand weapon executes a three (3) strike combination. Starting from the left side with the left-hand weapon, execute an Inward Low target to your opponent's right knee. With your right-hand weapon, which is chambered on top of your left forearm, execute a right back hand low strike to your opponent's right knee. Now chambered on your right side in the "**Aldabis**" strike position from after the first left hand strike, execute a left Back Hand Low target to your opponent's left knee.

Note: While executing this Inward Low, Back Hand Low and Back Hand Low drill as you both target one another's target area, your weapons will hit each other forming an "X" at each height Low, Low and Low. This drill sequence can be repeated several times, depending on the instructor, and can be performed in a stationary "**De Fondo**" stance or in a "**Luton**" flowing foot work as you change into either right foot lead or into a left foot lead stance while each time adjusting your rear leg and foot in a "**Columpio**" manner.

10. "Salot Saboy, Sombrada" Scoop and Throw with Roof Block

This technique is an Upward Six Striking Pattern that is referred as **"Salat Saboy"** meaning shoulder and hip respectively but the true meaning or the romantic Filipino reference as applied to Escrima is **"Scoop and Throw."** Just picture yourself scooping in a bag of rice seeds hanging at your hips and grabbing the seeds in your hand launching the seeds into the air. This technique is based on the principle of Inward Low, Back Hand Low and Back Hand Low. This technique is a three (3) strike pattern weaving combinations right and left consisting of Low, Low, Low all traveling upwards in a diagonal direction consisting of **"Saboy, "Aldabis", "Aldabis** with **"Sombrada"** striking combinations on each side and a Roof block associated with every third strike. While in a left foot lead, **"Laban Handa"** stance or **"Mandirigma"** stance, with both of your weapons chambered at each side pointing upwards in a vertical position ready to parry, defend or attack, step forward into a right foot lead stance and execute the Inward low **"Saboy"** strike starting with the right-hand weapon. The strike is to your opponent's left knee. As you are executing this inward low line strike and stepping forward with your right foot, chamber your left-hand weapon on top of your right forearm with the cutting edge of your sword facing your opponent. Note: this action of stepping forward and chambering your left-hand weapon on top of your right forearm is in reality a parry, block or strike. You do not simply chamber your left-hand weapon over on top your right forearm, because it will completely expose your left side open for a counter strike. You simply step into the chamber after a left-hand weapon parry, block, or strike as you execute the first inward low line **"Saboy"** strike with your right-hand weapon to your opponent's left knee. Then immediately follow with a back hand low **"Aldabis"** strike with the left-hand weapon that is chambered on top of the right forearm to your opponent's left knee and immediately followed with a back hand low "**Aldabis**" strike with the right-hand weapon to your opponent's right knee. At this same moment in time, chamber your left-hand weapon over your head to execute a Roof Block or **"Sombrada"**. This added Roof Block technique will protect your head from any high line counter strike from your opponent as you attack the lower target areas of your opponent. Once the first three (3) series of strikes with Roof Block are completed from the right foot lead stance, chamber your right-hand weapon over your left forearm and swing **"Columpio"** your right foot back and step forward with your left foot into a left foot lead stance. Execute the inward low **"Saboy"** strike from the left-hand weapon that is in the Roof Block position over your head. Rotate your weapon counterclockwise around your head in a **"Sinalakot"** manner to your opponent's right knee. As you are executing this inward low line strike and stepping forward with your left foot, chamber your right-hand weapon over your left forearm with the cutting edge of your sword facing your opponent. Note: This action of stepping forward and chambering your right-hand weapon on top of your right forearm is in reality a parry, block, or strike. Again, you do not simply chamber your right-hand weapon on top your right forearm, because it will completely expose your right side open for a counter strike. You simply step into the chamber after a right-hand weapon parry, block, or strike as you execute the first inward low line **"Saboy"** strike with your right-hand weapon to your opponent's right knee. Immediately follow with a back hand low **"Aldabis"** strike with the right-hand weapon that is chambered on top of the right forearm to your opponent's right knee and immediately followed with a back hand low **"Aldabis"** strike with the left-hand weapon to your opponent's left knee. At this same moment in time, chamber your right-hand weapon over your head to execute a Roof Block or **"Sombrada."** This added Roof Block technique will protect your head from any high line counter strike from your opponent as you attack the lower target areas of your opponent. Once the first three (3) series of strikes with Roof Block are completed from the left foot lead stance, chamber your left-hand weapon on top of your left forearm, you will now swing, **"Columpio,"** your left foot back and step forward with your right foot into a right foot lead stance, completing the **"Salot Saboy con Sombrada"** Six strike series. The Salot Saboy with Roof Block Six Inward Low, Back Hand Low and Back Hand Low with Roof Block is divided up into three (3) target strike areas and is sometimes called Low, Low, Low or (L, L, L) consisting of three (3) strikes per side of Saboy, Aldabis, Aldabis with a Roof Block.

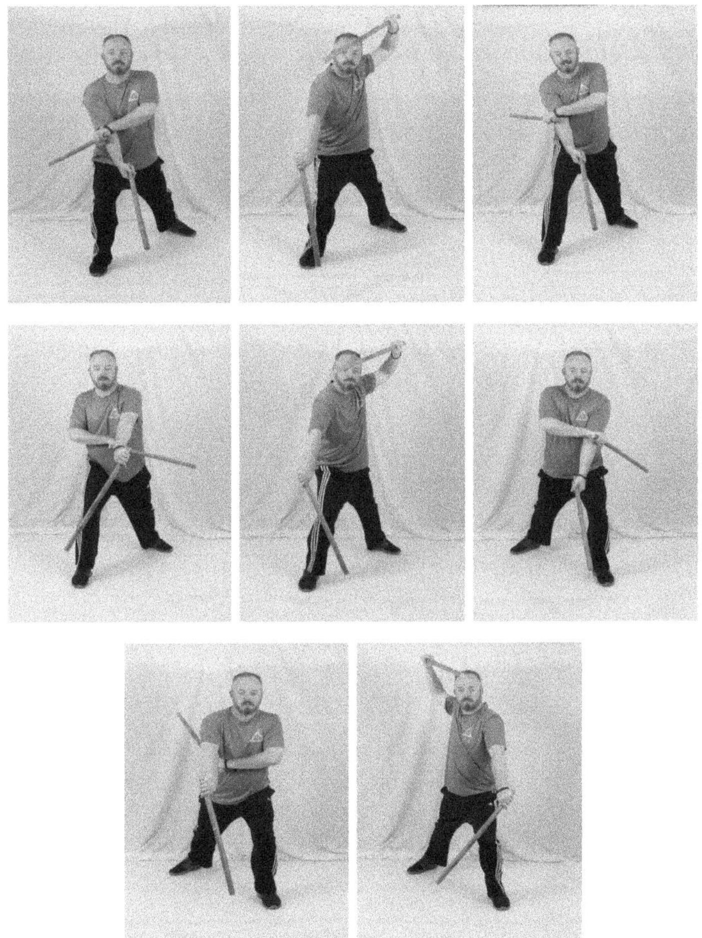

"Sombrada" or partner Drill for "Salot Saboy, Sombrada" Scoop and Throw with Roof Block Drill

1. The right-hand weapon executes a three (3) strike combination. Starting from the right side with the right-hand weapon, execute an Inward Low target to your opponent's left knee. With your left-hand weapon, which is chambered on top of your right forearm, execute a left-hand Back Hand

Low target to your opponent's left knee. Now chambered on your left side in the "**Aldabis**" strike position after the first right hand strike, execute a right-hand Back Hand Low target to your opponent's right knee. At the same time execute a Roof Block over your head with your left-hand weapon.

2. The left-hand weapon executes a three (3) strike combination. Starting from the left side with the left-hand weapon, execute an Inward Low target to your opponent's right knee. With your right-hand weapon, which is chambered over your head in the Roof Block position, rotate your weapon clockwise back around your head in a "**Sinalakot**" manner down to your left side "**Saboy**" strike position. Execute your first second series Inward Low target to your opponent's right knee. Then execute a right Back Hand Low target to your opponent's right knee. Now, chambered on your right side in the "**Aldabis**" strike position from after the first left hand strike, execute a low left back hand strike targeting your opponent's left knee. At the same time, execute a roof block over your head with your right-hand weapon.

Note: While executing this Inward Low, Back Hand Low and Back Hand Low with Roof Block drill, you both target one another's target area. Your weapons will hit each other forming an "X" at each height Low, Low and Low with Roof Block. This drill sequence can be repeated several times depending on the instructor and can be performed in a stationary "**De Fondo**" stance or in a "**Luton**" flowing foot work. As you change into either right foot lead or left foot lead stance, adjusting your rear leg and foot in a "Columpia" manner.

11. "Redonda" or "Redondo"

The "**Redonda**" circular striking Sinawali pattern is very similar to "**Cielo Seis**" or Heaven Six striking and chambering, but now your target area is all concentrated on one specific target. The word "**Redonda**" in Chabacano and Spanish means a pasture, or large field, or even region. "**Redondo**" means round, or a large circular ring, but the romantic Filipino meaning of "**Redonda**" or "**Redondo**" in Filipino Arnis is applied to a fast circular strike like a whirlwind or tornado. The "Redonda" technique can be targeted to any target area of your opponent's body High Line, Mid-Line, and Low Line target areas that become open during a combat confrontation for a strike or counter strike. Your body position in relationship to your opponent will only allow you to concentrate on a brief window of opportunity to execute or deliver a strike to one specific open area of your opponent. With the "**Redonda**" technique and other "**Redonda**" techniques to follow, it will be very beneficial to a practitioner of Filipino Arnis/Escrima/Kali to know these techniques in order to effectively engage your opponent from an awkward position or stance as you are limited to only one open target area at that moment. For purposes and illustration of this technique as related in this book your target area will be the center line of your opponent's head or face. It is encouraged that you practice other target areas so that you will become proficient in executing this technique. While in a left foot lead, **"Laban Handa"** stance or **"Mandirigma"** stance, with both of your weapons chambered at each side pointing upwards in a vertical position ready to parry, defend, or attack, step forward into a right foot lead stance. Execute the Inward high strike starting with the right-hand weapon. The target is your opponent's face. As you are executing this inward high line strike and stepping forward with your right foot, chamber your left-hand weapon under your right armpit with the cutting edge of your sword facing your opponent. Note: This action of stepping forward and chambering your left-hand weapon under your right armpit is in reality a parry, block, or strike, as mentioned before in other techniques. Then, immediately follow with a back hand high strike with the left-hand weapon that is chambered under the right arm pit with the same target area to your opponent's face. Immediately follow with the right-hand weapon, which is now chambered on your left side near your left shoulder, and the target area is your opponent's face. This third strike is executed by rotating your right-hand wrist counterclockwise in a quick whipping action called **"Cola de Lagarto,"** or tail of the lizard, inward strike to your opponent's face. The **"Cola de Lagarto"** wiping action strike generates power, and this third inward strike is now an accentuated with power. Once the first three (3) series of strikes are completed from the right foot lead stance, chamber your right-hand weapon under your left armpit. You will now swing, **"Columpio,"** your right foot back and step forward with your left foot into a left foot lead stance. Now that you are in a left foot lead stance, execute the Inward high strike. Starting with the left-hand weapon, target your opponent's face. As you are executing this inward high line strike and stepping forward with your left foot, chamber your right-hand weapon under your left armpit with the cutting edge of your sword facing your opponent. Then, immediately follow with a back hand high strike with the right-hand weapon that is chambered under the left arm pit to the same target area of the first strike, which is your opponent's face. Immediately follow with the left-hand weapon, which is now chambered on your right side near your right shoulder, and the target area is your opponent's face. This third strike from the left foot lead stance is executed by rotating your left-hand wrist clockwise in a quick wiping action called **"Cola de Lagarto,"** or tail of the lizard, inward strike to your opponent's face. Once the second three (3) series of strikes are completed from the left foot lead stance, chamber your left-hand weapon under your right armpit. You will now swing, **"Columpio,"** your left foot back and step forward with your right foot into a right foot lead stance, completing the "Redonda" six strike series to one target area. The **"Redonda"** Six Inward High, Back Hand High and Inward Hand High is divided up into three (3) target strike areas and is sometimes called High, High, High or (H, H, H) consisting of three (3) strikes per side. This technique can be executed Middle, Middle, Middle, or (M, M, M) and Low, Low, Low or (L, L, L).

"Sombrada" or Partner Drill for "Redonda" Drill

1. The right-hand weapon executes a three (3) strike combination. Starting from the right side with the right-hand weapon, execute an Inward High target to your opponent's face at centerline. With your left-hand weapon, which is chambered under your right arm pit, execute a high left-hand back hand strike targeting your opponent's face. Now chambered on your left side in the No. 2 **"Bartical"** strike position from after the first right hand strike, execute a right High Inward strike by using the **"Cola de Lagarto"** counterclockwise wrist rotation and strike your opponent's face.

2. The left-hand weapon executes a three (3) strike combination starting from the left side. With the left-hand weapon, execute a high inward strike targeting your opponent's face at centerline. With your right-hand weapon, which is chambered under your left arm pit, execute a high right back hand strike targeting your opponent's face. Now chambered on your right side in the No. 2 **"Bartical"** strike position from after the first left hand strike, execute a left High inward strike by using the **"Cola de Lagarto"** clockwise wrist rotation and strike your opponent's face.

Note: While executing this Inward High, Back Hand High with Inward wrist rotation Hand High drill, you and your partner both target one another's target area. Your weapons will hit each other forming an "X" at each height High, High and High. This drill sequence can be repeated several times depending on the instructor and can be performed in a stationary **"De Fondo"** stance or in a **"Luton"** flowing foot work as you change into either right foot lead or into a left foot lead stance while each time adjusting your rear leg and foot in a **"Columpio"** manner.

12. "Rapido Redonda" Fast Rapid strikes with circular striking pattern

The "**Rapido Redonda**" circular striking Sinawali pattern is very similar to the "**Redonda**" striking pattern, but now you will prefix it with two inward rapid multiple strikes in the sinawali pattern, simply adding, or augmenting, the sinawali route into a new pattern. The target area for this technique is all concentrated on one specific target. The word "Rapido" in Chabacano and Spanish means fast or rapid like motion. The romantic Filipino meaning of "**Rapido Redonda**" or "**Rapido Redondo**" in Filipino Arnis/Escrima/Kali is applied to fast multiple strikes followed with circular strikes, like a whirlwind or tornado. The "**Rapido Redonda**" technique can be targeted to any area of your opponent's body High Line, Mid-Line, and Low Line target areas that become open during a combat confrontation for a strike or counter strike. Furthermore, your body position in relationship to your opponent will only allow you to only concentrate on a brief window of opportunity to execute or deliver a strike to one specific open area of your opponent. For purposes and illustration of this technique as related in this book, your target area will be the center line of your opponent's head or face. It is encouraged that you practice other target areas so that you will become proficient in executing this technique. From a left foot lead **"Laban Handa"** stance or **"Mandirigma,"** stance with both of your weapons chambered at each side pointing upwards in a vertical position ready to parry, defend, or attack, execute two rapid inward vertical strikes to your opponent's face at centerline. The right-hand weapon is in the **"Abierta,"** open, chambered position and the left-hand weapon is in the "Cerrada," closed, chambered position. You will strike in a quick, rapid scissor-like motion in succession of each other. Then step forward into a right foot lead stance and swing **"Columpio"** your left foot to be adjusted directly behind your right foot lead stance and execute the Inward high strike starting with the right-hand weapon target is to your opponent's face. As you are executing this inward high line strike and stepping forward with your right foot, chamber your left-hand weapon under your right armpit with the cutting edge of your sword facing your opponent. Note: this action of stepping forward and chambering your left-hand weapon under your right armpit is in reality a strike after the rapid left hand strike prefix. Immediately follow with a back hand high strike with the left-hand weapon that is chambered under the right arm pit to the same target area to your opponent's face. Immediately follow with the right-hand weapon, which is now chambered on your left side near your left shoulder, and the target area is your opponent's face. This fifth strike is executed by rotating your right-hand wrist counterclockwise in a quick wiping action called **"Cola de Lagarto,"** or tail of the lizard, inward strike to your opponent's face. The **"Cola de Lagarto"** wiping action strike generates power, and this third inward strike is now accentuated with power. Once the first five (5) series of strikes are completed from the right side, chamber both of your weapons at each side with your weapons pointing upwards in a vertical position ready to parry, defend or attack. Execute two rapid inward vertical strikes to your opponent's face at centerline first with the left hand weapon from the **"Abierta"** open chambered position and then with the right hand weapon from the **"Cerrada"** closed chambered position in a quick, rapid scissor like motion in succession of each other. As you are chambering your right hand weapon under your left armpit, you will now swing **"Columpio"** your right foot back and step forward with your left foot into a left foot lead stance. Note: The continuous **"Columpio"** action of rhythmically swinging and adjusting your foot work into a different stance from one side to the other side is the same **"Luton"** foot work as mentioned before, like in the dancing style known as "**Estilo de Salon**". Now, execute the high inward strike. Starting with the left-hand weapon, the target is to your opponent's face. As you are executing this inward high line strike and stepping forward with your left foot, chamber your right-hand weapon under your left armpit with the cutting edge of your sword facing your opponent. Then immediately follow with a back hand high strike with the right-hand weapon that is chambered under the left arm pit to the same target area of the first strike, which is your opponent's face. Immediately follow with the left-hand weapon, which is now chambered on your right side near, your right shoulder, and the target area is your opponent's face. This third strike from the left foot lead stance is executed by rotating your left-hand wrist clockwise in a quick wiping action called **"Cola de Lagarto,"** or tail of the lizard, inward strike to your opponent's face. Once the second five (5) series of strikes are completed from the left side swing **"Columpio,"** put your left foot back and step forward with your right foot into a right foot lead, completing the "Rapido Redonda" ten (10) strike series to one target area. Your weapons are now chambered on each side in a vertical position ready to parry, block, or strike. The "**Rapido Redonda**" Ten (10) Inward High, Back Hand High and Inward Hand High, Back hand High and Inward hand High is divided up into five (5) target strike areas and is sometimes called High, High, High, High, High or H, H, H, H, H consisting of five (5) strikes per side. This technique can be executed Middle, Middle, Middle, Middle, Middle or M, M, M, M, M and Low, Low, Low, Low, Low or L, L, L, L, L.

"Sombrada" or Partner Drill for "Rapido Redonda"

1. The right-hand weapon executes a five (5) strike combination. Starting from the right side with the right-hand weapon, execute a high inward strike targeting your opponent's face. Immediately follow with an inward left strike to your opponent's face at centerline. Immediately chamber your left-hand weapon under your right arm pit as you step in and execute a right inward strike to your opponent's face and follow with a left back hand strike to your opponent's face. Now chambered on your left side in the No. 2 **"Bartical"** strike position from after the first right hand strike, execute a right high inward strike by using the **"Cola de Lagarto"** counterclockwise wrist rotation and strike your opponent's face.

2. The left-hand weapon executes a five (5) strike combination. Starting from the left side with the left-hand weapon, execute a left hand inward high target to your opponent's face. Immediately follow with a right-hand inward strike to your opponent's face at centerline and then chamber your right-hand weapon under your left arm pit as you step in and execute a left inward strike to your opponent's face. Immediately follow with a right back hand strike to your opponent's face. Now chambered on your right side in the No. 2 **"Bartical"** strike position from after the first right hand strike, execute a right High Inward strike by using the **"Cola de Lagarto"** clockwise wrist rotation and strike your opponent's face.

Note: While executing this Inward High, Back Hand High and Inward High, Back Hand High wrist rotation Hand High drill as you both target one another's target area; your weapons will hit each other forming an "X" at each height High, High and High, High, High. This drill sequence can be repeated several times depending on the instructor and can be performed in a stationary "**De Fondo**" stance or in a "**Luton**" flowing foot work as you change into either right foot lead or into a left foot lead stance while each time adjusting your rear leg and foot in a "**Columpio**" manner.

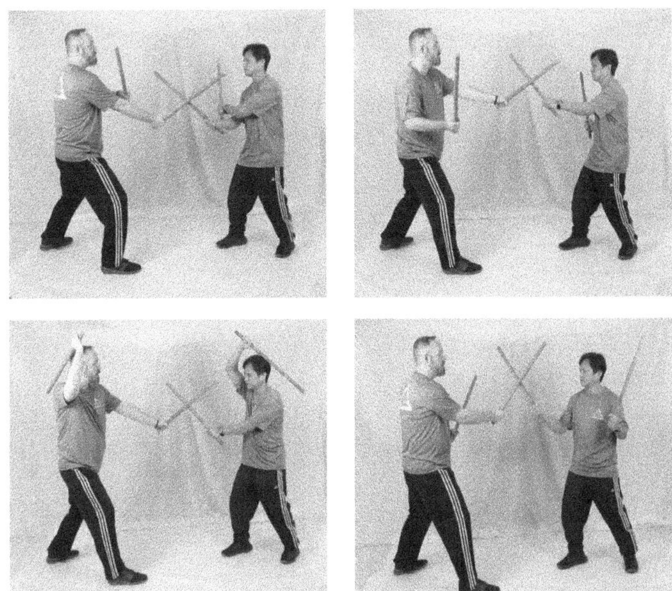

13. "Gemelo Abanico, Cielo Seis" or "Kambal Abanico, Langit"

This technique has the expression "**Abanico**" in it, but really the technique is a 360 degree "**Redonda**" that resembles a circular fan motion overhead. It literally means "Twin Fans with Heaven six sinawali striking pattern combination". This technique is based on the principle of Inward High, Back Hand High, Redonda, Inward High, Back Hand High and Back Hand High. This technique has a Filipino romantic expression for five (5) high line striking weaving combinations right and left per each side with an alternating twin fan/ "**Redonda**" heavy circular strike. While in a left foot lead "**Laban Handa**" stance or "**Mandirigma**" stance with both of your weapons chambered at each side pointing upwards in a vertical position ready to parry, defend, or attack, step forward into a right foot lead stance and execute the inward high strike starting with the right-hand weapon.

The target is to your opponent's left temple, neck, or shoulder. As you are executing this inward high line strike and stepping forward with your right foot, chamber your left-hand weapon under your right armpit with the cutting edge of your sword facing your opponent. Note: This action of stepping forward and chambering your left-hand weapon under your right armpit is in reality a parry, block or strike. You do not simply chamber your left-hand weapon under your right armpit, because it will completely expose your left side for a counter strike. You simply step into the chamber after a left-hand weapon parry, block, or strike. You execute the first inward high line strike with your right-hand weapon. Then immediately rotate your inward high strike around your head counterclockwise, and as you are rotating your weapon, follow with a back hand high strike with the left-hand weapon that is chambered under the right arm pit with the same target area of the first strike. After this back hand strike, immediately chamber back to the same chambered position, under your right armpit. Now from the rotating right-hand weapon going around your head in a counterclockwise circular fan/redonda motion, execute the same target area as before which is your opponent's left temple, neck, or left shoulder. Again, execute the left-hand back hand with the left-hand weapon, which is now chambered under your right armpit, and strike your opponent's right temple, neck, or shoulder. After this strike your right-hand weapon should now be chambered near your left shoulder, and now execute a back hand strike to your opponent's right temple, neck, or shoulder. Once the first five (5) series of strikes are completed from the right foot lead stance, chamber your right-hand weapon under your left armpit. You will now swing **"Columpio"** your right back and step forward with your left foot into a left foot lead stance. Now that you are in a left foot lead stance, execute the inward high strike starting with the left-hand weapon targeting your opponent's right temple, neck, or shoulder. As you are executing this inward high line strike, chamber your right-hand weapon under your right armpit with the cutting edge of your sword facing your opponent. Then immediately rotate your inward high strike around your head clockwise, and as you are rotating your weapon, follow with a back hand high strike with the right-hand weapon that is chambered under the left arm pit with the same target area of the first strike. After this back hand strike, immediately chamber back to the same chambered position, under your left armpit. Now from the rotating left-hand weapon going around your head in a clockwise circular fan/"**Redonda**" motion, execute the same target area as before, which is your opponent's right temple, neck, or shoulder. Again, execute the right-hand back hand with the right-hand weapon, which is now chambered under your left armpit, and strike your opponent's right temple, neck, or shoulder. After this strike, your right-hand weapon should now be chambered near your right shoulder. Now, execute a back hand strike to your opponent's left temple, neck, or shoulder. Once the second five (5) series of strikes are completed from the left foot lead stance as you are chambering your left-hand weapon under your right armpit, you will now swing **"Columpio"** your left foot back and step forward with your right foot into a right foot lead stance. Now that you are in a right foot lead stance this will complete the full ten (10) count striking pattern.

The "**Gemelo Abanico, Cielo Seis**" or "**Kambal Abanico, Langit**", Ten (10) count High, Back Hand High, Redonda Inward High, Back Hand High and Back Hand High is divided up into five (5) target strike areas and is sometimes called High, High, High, High, High or H, H, H, H, H consisting of five (5) strikes per side. This technique can be executed Middle, Middle, Middle, Middle, Middle, or M, M, M, M, M and Low, Low, Low, Low, Low or L, L, L, L, L.

Sombrada for "Gemelo Abanico, Cielo Seis" or "Kambal Abanico, Langit" Drill:

1. The right-hand weapon executes a five (5) strike combination. Starting from the right side with the right-hand weapon, execute a high inward strike, targeting your opponent's left temple and strike through as you "**Redonda**" rotate 360 degrees around your head counterclockwise. As you are in the process of rotating your "**Redonda**" around your head with your left hand weapon, which is chambered under your right arm pit, execute a left hand back hand high strike targeting your opponent's left temple. Chamber back to the original chambered position under your right armpit and immediately follow with the "Redonda" strike to your opponent's left temple. Strike through again and chamber your right-hand weapon on your left side in the No. 2 "**Bartical**" strike position from after the second right hand inward rotating "**Redonda**" strike, and execute a left hand back hand high strike targeting your opponent's left temple. Immediately follow with a right-hand back hand strike to your opponent's right temple.

2. The left-hand weapon executes a five (5) strike combination. Starting from the left side with the left-hand weapon, execute an inward high strike, targeting your opponent's right temple and strike through as you "Redonda" rotate 360 degrees around your head clockwise. As you are in the process of rotating your "Redonda" around your head with your right-hand weapon, which is chambered under your left arm pit, execute a high right-hand back hand strike, targeting to your opponent's right temple. Chamber back to the original chambered position under your left armpit.

Immediately follow with the **"Redonda"** strike to your opponent's right temple and strike through again. Chamber your right-hand weapon on your right side in the No. 2 **"Bartical"** strike position from after the second left-hand inward rotating **"Redonda"** strike and execute a high right-hand back hand strike, targeting your opponent's right temple. Immediately follow with a left-hand back hand strike to your opponent's left temple.

14. "Gemelo Abanico, Cielo y Tierra Seis" or "Kambal Abanico, Langit at Lupa"

This technique is very similar to the previous technique and has the expression **"Abanico"** in it. However, the technique is really a 360 degree **"Redonda"** that resembles a circular fan motion overhead. It means "Twin Fan with Heaven and Earth six sinawali striking pattern combination". This technique is based on the principle of Inward High, Back Hand Low, Redonda, Inward High, Back Hand Low and Back Hand High. This technique has a Filipino romantic expression for five (5) high line striking right or left weaving combinations, High and Low strikes per each side, with an alternating twin fan/redonda heavy circular strike. While in a left foot lead, **"Laban Handa"** stance or **"Mandirigma"** stance, with both of your weapons chambered at each side, pointing upwards in a vertical position ready to parry, defend, or attack, step forward into a right foot lead stance. While stepping into a right foot lead, execute a high inward strike starting with the right-hand weapon, targeting your opponent's left temple, neck, or shoulder. As you are executing this high inward strike and stepping forward with your right foot, chamber your left-hand weapon under your right armpit with the cutting edge of your sword facing your opponent. Then, immediately rotate your inward high strike around your head counterclockwise, and as you are rotating your weapon, follow with a back hand low strike with the left-hand weapon that is chambered under the right arm pit to your opponent's left knee. After this back hand low strike, immediately chamber back to the same chambered position, under your right armpit. Now, from the rotating right-hand weapon going around your head in a counterclockwise circular fan/redonda motion, execute the same target area as before, which is your opponent's left temple, neck, or shoulder. Again, execute the left-hand back hand with the left-hand weapon, which is now chambered in your right armpit, and strike your opponent's right knee. After this strike, your right-hand weapon should now be chambered near your left shoulder. Execute a back hand strike to your opponent's right temple, neck, or shoulder. Once the first five (5) series of strikes are completed from the right foot lead stance, as you are chambering your right-hand weapon under your left armpit, you will now swing **"Columpio"** your right foot back and step forward with your left foot into a left foot lead stance. Now that you are in a left foot lead stance, execute the inward high strike starting with the left-hand weapon, targeting your opponent's right temple, neck, or shoulder. As you are executing this inward high line strike and stepping forward with your left foot, chamber your right-hand weapon under your left armpit, with the cutting edge of your sword facing your opponent. Then, immediately rotate your inward high strike around your head clockwise, and as you are rotating your weapon, follow with a back hand low strike with the right-hand weapon that is chambered under the left arm pit. Strike your opponent's right knee, and after this back hand strike, immediately chamber back to the same chambered position, under your left armpit. Now, from the rotating left-hand weapon going around your head in a clockwise circular fan/ **"Redonda"** motion, execute the same target area as before, which is your opponent's right temple, neck, or shoulder. Again, execute the right hand back strike with the right-hand weapon, which is now chambered on your left armpit, and strike your opponent's right knee. After this strike, your left-hand weapon should now be chambered near your right shoulder. Now execute a back hand strike to your opponent's left temple, neck, or shoulder. Once the second five (5) series of strikes are completed from the left foot lead stance, chamber your left-hand weapon under your right armpit. You will now swing **"Columpio"** your left foot back and step forward with your right foot into a right foot lead stance. Now that you are back in a right foot lead stance, this will complete the full ten (10) count striking pattern. The **"Gemelo Abanico, Cielo y Tierra Seis"** or **"Kambal Abanico, Langit at Lupa"**, Ten (10) count Inward High, Back Hand Low, Redonda Inward High, Back Hand Low and Back Hand High is divided up into five (5) target strike areas and is sometimes called High, Low, High, Low, High or H, L, H, L, H consisting of five (5) strikes per side.

Sombrada for "Gemelo Abanico, Cielo y Tierra Seis" or "Kambal Abanico, Langit at Lupa" Drill:

1. The right-hand weapon executes a five (5) strike combination. Starting from the right side with the right-hand weapon, execute a high inward strike targeting your opponent's left temple and strike through as you "Redonda" rotate 360 degrees around your head counterclockwise. As you are in the process of executing the rotating "Redonda" around your head with your left-hand weapon, which is chambered under your right arm pit, execute a left-hand back hand low target to your opponent's left knee, and chamber back to the original chambered position under your right armpit. Immediately follow with the "Redonda" strike to your opponent's left temple and strike through again. Chamber your right-hand weapon on your left side in the No. 2 "Bartical" strike and execute a left-hand back hand low target to your opponent's left knee. Immediately follow with a right-hand back hand strike to your opponent's right temple.

2. The left-hand weapon executes a five (5) strike combination. Starting from the left side with the left-hand weapon, execute a high inward strike targeting your opponent's right temple, and strike through as you "Redonda" rotate 360 degrees around your head clockwise. As you are in the process of executing the rotating "Redonda" around your head with your right-hand weapon, which is chambered under your left arm pit, execute a right-hand back hand high target to your opponent's right knee and chamber back to the original chambered position under your left armpit. Immediately follow with the "**Redonda**" strike to your opponent's right temple and strike through again. Chamber your right-hand weapon on your right side in the No. 2 **"Bartical"** strike position and execute a right-hand back hand low target to your opponent's right knee. Immediately follow with a left-hand back hand strike to your opponent's left temple.

15. "Salida del Sol, Redonda Salot Saboy"

This Sinawali Striking Pattern combination means early morning sunrise with circular upwards scooping strikes. It has a romantic Filipino reference as applied to Escrima with the early morning sunshine reflecting off the two blades in motion as they seem to sparkle against the rays of the sun light. This technique is in reality a combination of the 5th and 9th or "**Kaluban** and **Salot Saboy**" techniques previously described. While in a left foot lead **"Laban Handa"** stance or **"Mandirigma"** stance with both of your weapons chambered at each side pointing upwards in a vertical position ready to parry, defend, or attack, step forward into a right foot lead stance. As you are stepping into the right foot lead stance, execute with your right-hand weapon a **"Taga"** strike across your opponent's torso. At the same time, with your left-hand weapon, you will execute a **"Saboy"** strike across your opponent's torso. Note: The right-hand weapon should be on top of your left-hand weapon as you execute this double diagonal slashes. Once both inward diagonal slashes are completed, your hands should be crossed at the center line of your opponent's mid-section. Then, immediately rotate your right-hand weapon counterclockwise and your left-hand weapon clockwise. With this rotating action, your cutting edges of your swords will be positioned for the diagonal shearing action as you draw the swords simultaneously out to the **"Abierta,"** open, position while executing a double shearing cut against your opponent's torso. As the action of the shearing and drawing of the swords is being executed, you should adjust and swing your right foot back so that you will now again be in a left foot lead, **"Laban Handa"** stance or **"Mandirigma"** stance. Step forward into a right foot lead stance and execute the low **"Saboy"** strike starting with the right-hand weapon targeting your opponent's left knee. As you execute this inward low line strike and are stepping forward with your right foot, chamber your left-hand weapon on top of your right forearm with the cutting edge of your sword facing your opponent. Then, step as you execute the first low line **"Saboy"** strike with your right-hand weapon to your opponent's left knee. Immediately follow with a low **"Aldabis"** strike with the left-hand weapon that is chambered on top of the right forearm to your opponent's left knee. Follow with a low **"Aldabis"** strike with the right-hand weapon to your opponent's right knee. Once the scooping upward series of strikes are completed from the right foot lead stance, step forward with your left so that you will be in a left foot lead stance. As you are in the left foot lead stance, execute with your left-hand weapon a **"Taga"** strike across your opponent's torso. At the same time, with your right-hand weapon, execute a **"Saboy"** strike across your opponent's torso. Note: the left-hand weapon should be on top of your right-hand weapon as you execute this double diagonal slashes. Once both inward diagonal slashes are completed, both hands should be crossed at the center line of your opponent's mid-section. Then, immediately rotate your left-hand weapon clockwise and your right-hand weapon counterclockwise; with this rotating action your cutting edges of your swords will be positioned for the diagonal shearing action as you draw the swords simultaneously out to the **"Abierta,"** open, position while executing a double shearing cut against your opponent's torso. As the action of the shearing and drawing of the swords is being executed, you should adjust and swing your left foot back so that you will now be in a right foot lead, **"Laban Handa"** stance or **"Mandirigma"** stance. Now step forward with your left foot into a left foot lead stance and execute the inward low **"Saboy"** strike starting with the left-hand weapon targeting your opponent's right knee. As you are executing this inward low line **"Saboy"** strike and stepping forward with your left foot, chamber your right-hand weapon on top of your left forearm with the cutting edge of your sword facing your opponent. Note: this action of stepping forward and chambering your right-hand weapon on top of your left forearm is in reality a parry, block or strike as you execute the first inward low line **"Saboy"** strike with your left-hand weapon to your opponent's right knee. Then, immediately follow with a back hand low **"Aldabis"** strike with the right-hand weapon that is chambered on top of the left forearm to your opponent's right knee and immediately follow with a back hand low "Aldabis" strike with the left-hand weapon to your opponent's left knee. Once the second upward scooping strike series of **"Saboy", "Aldabis", "Aldabis"** strikes are completed from the left foot lead stance as you are chambering your left-hand weapon on top of your right forearm, you will now swing **"Columpio"** your left foot back and step forward with your right foot into a right foot lead stance, completing the **"Salida del Sol, Redonda Salot Saboy"** sinawali striking pattern.

"Salida del Sol, Redonda Salot Saboy" Drill:

This is a two-person drill with both persons facing off one another directly while in a left foot lead **"Laban Handa"** stance or **"Mandirigma"** stance. Note: the first part of this drill is difficult to have both you and your training partner striking one another's weapons. For this first part of the drill, it is best to position yourselves into a "Largo Mano" distance so that your weapons will not touch or strike each other. Just step into each striking position in mirror of each other and step out backwards. Visualize cutting your opponent's torso diagonally as you execute the double sword shearing action. Then, for the second part of the drill, you can both step in and have your weapons striking each other at the centerline forming an "X" as you execute the upward scooping **"Saboy,"** **"Aldabis,"** and **"Aldabis"** strikes.

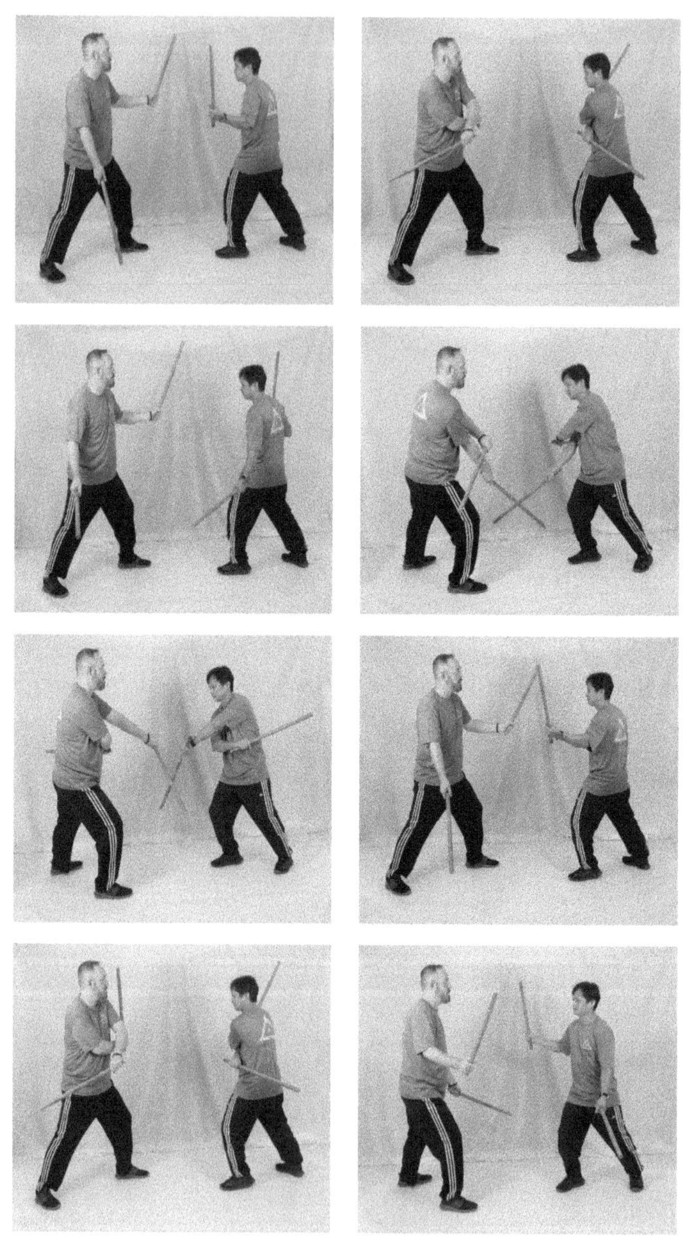

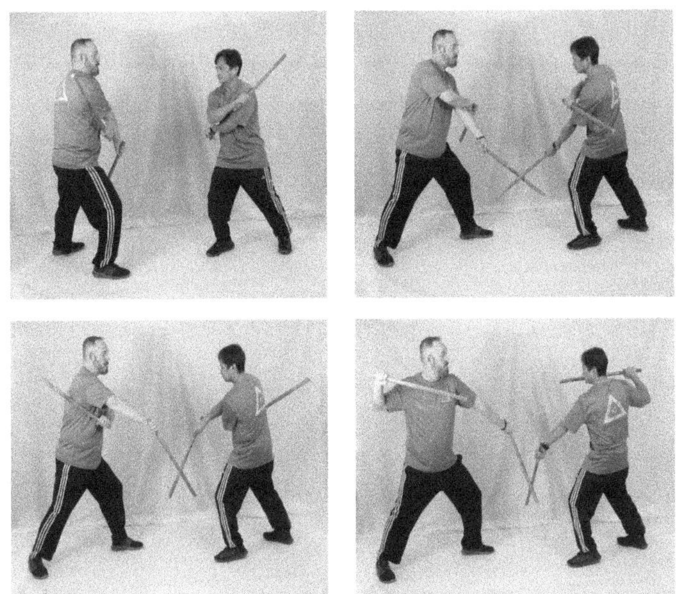

16. "Cola de Lagarto"

This Sinawali Striking Pattern combination means "The Tail of the Lizard" with circular upwards scooping strikes and quick reversal to downward descending strikes. It has a romantic Filipino reference as applied to Escrima with a wiping motion of a Lizard's tail as you reverse direction of your blades in rapid secession. This technique is in reality a combination of the 5th, 9th, and 7th or "**Kaluban, Salot Saboy,** and **Cielo Seis**" techniques previously described. While in a left foot lead, **"Laban Handa"** stance or **"Mandirigma"** stance, with both of your weapons chambered at each side pointing upwards in a vertical position ready to parry, defend, or attack, step forward into a right foot lead stance. As you are stepping into the right foot lead stance, execute with your right-hand weapon a **"Taga"** strike across your opponent's torso. At the same time, with you left hand weapon, you will execute an **"Saboy"** strike across your opponent's torso. Note: the right-hand weapon should be on top of your left-hand weapon as you execute these double diagonal slashes. Once both inward diagonal slashes are completed, your hands should be crossed at the center line of your opponent's mid-section. Then, immediately rotate your right-hand weapon counterclockwise and your left-hand weapon clockwise. With this rotating action, your cutting edges of your swords will be positioned for the diagonal shearing action as you draw the swords simultaneously out to the **"Abierta,"** open, position while executing a double shearing diagonal cut against your opponent's torso. As the action of the shearing and drawing of the swords is being executed, you should adjust and swing your right foot back so that you will now again be in a left foot lead, **"Laban Handa"** stance or **"Mandirigma"** stance. Step forward into a right foot lead stance and execute the inward low **"Saboy"** strike. Starting with the right-hand weapon, target your opponent's right knee or any low target that maybe open. As you are executing this inward low line strike and stepping forward with your right foot, chamber your left-hand weapon on top of your right forearm with the cutting edge of your sword facing your opponent. Note: this action of stepping forward and chambering your left-hand weapon on top of your right forearm is in reality a parry, block or strike. You do not simply chamber your left-hand weapon on top your right forearm because it will completely expose your left side open for a counter strike. You simply step into the chamber after a left-hand weapon parry, block, or strike as you execute the first inward low line **"Saboy"** strike with your right-hand weapon to your opponent's left knee. Then, immediately follow with a back hand low **"Aldabis"** strike with the left-hand weapon that is chambered on top of the right forearm to your opponent's left knee. Immediately follow with a back hand low **"Aldabis"** strike with the right-hand weapon to your opponent's right knee. Now with your left-hand weapon chambered over your head as if you had executed a roof block, rotate your left-hand weapon clockwise as you change your right foot lead into a left foot lead stance. Begin the downward striking pattern of the second part of **"Cielo Seis"** of the 4th, 5th, and 6th strikes from your left side, striking your opponent's right temple, neck, or shoulder. Once the downward strikes are completed from the left foot lead stance, execute with your left-hand weapon a downward 45-degree diagonal **"Taga"** strike across your opponent's torso. At the same time, with your right-hand weapon, execute a **"Saboy"** strike across your opponent's torso. Note: the left-hand weapon should be on top of your right-hand weapon as you execute this double diagonal slashes. Once both inward diagonal slashes are completed, both hands should be crossed at the center line of your opponent's mid-section. Then, immediately rotate your left-hand weapon clockwise and your right-hand weapon counterclockwise. With this rotating action, the cutting edges of your swords will be positioned for the diagonal shearing action as you draw the swords simultaneously out to the **"Abierta,"** open, position executing a double shearing diagonal cut against your opponent's torso. As the action of the shearing and drawing of the swords is being executed, you should adjust and swing your left foot back so that you will now be in a right foot lead **"Laban Handa"** stance or **"Mandirigma"** stance. Step forward into a left foot lead stance and execute the inward low **"Saboy"** strike starting with the left-hand weapon targeting your opponent's right knee. As you are executing this inward low line strike and stepping forward with your left foot, chamber your right-hand weapon on top of your left forearm with the cutting edge of your sword facing your opponent. Then, as you are stepping, execute the first inward low line **"Saboy"** strike with your left-hand weapon to your opponent's left knee or any low target that maybe open. Then immediately follow with a back hand low **"Aldabis"** strike with the left-hand weapon that is chambered on top of the right forearm to your opponent's left knee. Immediately follow with a back hand low **"Aldabis"** strike with the right-hand weapon to your opponent's right knee. Next, with your left-hand weapon chambered over your head as if you had executed a roof block, rotate your left-hand weapon clockwise as you change your right foot lead to a left foot lead stance. Begin the downward striking pattern of the first part of "Cielo Seis" of the 1st, 2nd, and 3rd strikes from your right side, striking your opponent's left temple, neck, or shoulder. This will complete the series of strikes of the Sinawali technique of **"Cola de Lagarto"** or "Tail of the Lizard." Note: this technique should be executed in a rhythmically speedy manner, but first start out slow in order to build up speed and proficiency of executing this rapid action technique.

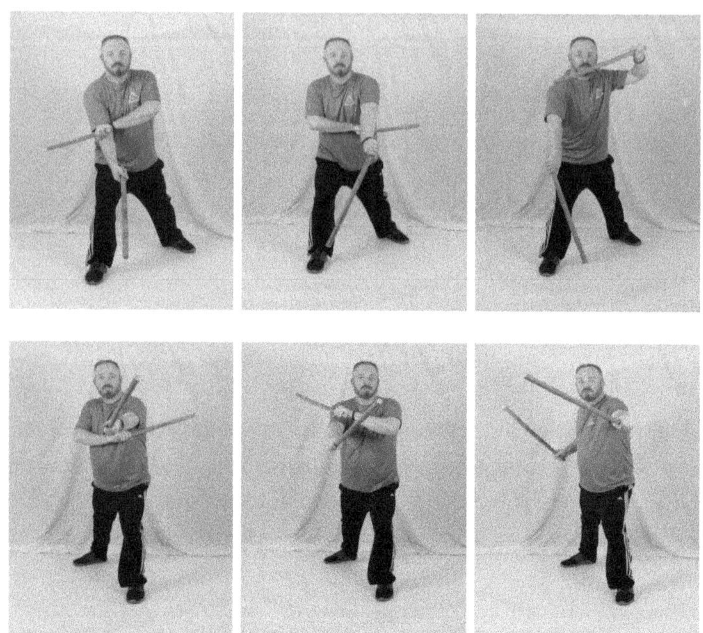

"Cola de Lagarto" Dril

This is a two-person drill with both persons directly facing off one another while in a left foot lead **"Laban Handa"** stance or **"Mandirigma"** stance. Note: the first part of this drill is difficult to have you and your training partner striking each other's weapons. For this first part of the drill, it is best to position yourselves into a **"Largo Mano"** distance so that your weapons will not touch or strike each other. Just step into each striking position in mirror of one another and step out backwards. Visualize cutting your opponent's torso diagonally as you execute the double sword shearing action. Then, for the second part of the drill, you can both step in and have your weapons striking each other at the centerline, forming an "X" as you execute the upward scooping **"Saboy"**, **"Aldabis"** and **"Aldabis"** strikes and the descending Inward, Back Hand, Back Hand strikes.

17. "Planchada Escalera"

This Sinawali Striking Pattern combination means to flatten, crisscross with ascending or descending steps but has a romantic Filipino reference in Escrima as a series of flat level horizontal strikes that either ascends upwards in equal increments or descends downward in equal increments on a level plane, as if one was going up or down a ladder or a flight of stairs. The motion of this sinawali technique is very similar to the 9th Sinawali technique known as **"Salot Saboy."** The strikes are a combination of a series of "**Planchada Abierta** and **Planchada Cerrada**" level strikes instead of upward scooping motion strikes. This technique is based on the principle of Inward level, Back Hand level and Back Hand level. This technique of three (3) strike weaving combination right and left consisting of Level, Level, Level all travel upwards or downwards in equal level divided increments consisting of "**Planchada Abierta**", "**Planchada Cerrada**", and "**Planchada Cerrada**" striking combinations on each side. From a normal stance with one's feet at 1 1/2 shoulder width apart and your weapons chambered at each side pointing upwards in a vertical position ready to parry, defend, or attack in an open body stance, face your opponent directly in front, which is called "**Abierta**." Pivot out on the balls of your feet with your left foot at 9 o'clock bending the left knee directly over the left toes with your right leg extended out straight at 3 o'clock, toes pointing forward 90 degrees, respective to the left foot. While in the process of pivoting your feet from this "abierta" stance, execute the Inward "**Planchada Abierta**" first (1ˢᵗ) strike with your right-hand weapon to the left side of your opponent's mid-section and follow with a back hand "**Planchada Cerrada**" second (2ⁿᵈ) strike with your left-hand weapon. The target is about three (3) inches lower than the first (1ˢᵗ) strike and immediately followed with a back hand "**Planchada Cerrada**" third (3ʳᵈ) strike with your right-hand weapon to your opponent's right side. The target is about three (3) inches lower than the second (2ⁿᵈ) strike. Now, pivot on the balls of your feet to the opposite side, your right foot at 3 o'clock bending the right knee directly over the right toes with your left leg extended out, straight at 9 o'clock, toes pointing forward 90 degrees, respective to the right foot. Again, while in the process of pivoting your feet from this "abierta" stance, execute the Inward "**Planchada Abierta**" fourth (4ᵗʰ) strike with your left-hand weapon to your opponent's right side, about three (3) inches lower than the previous third (3ʳᵈ) strike. Follow with a back hand "**Planchada Cerrada**" fifth (5ᵗʰ) strike with your right-hand weapon targeted about three (3) inches lower than the fourth (4ᵗʰ) strike and immediately follow with a back hand "Planchada Cerrada" sixth (6ᵗʰ) strike with your left-hand weapon to your opponent's left side about three (3) inches lower than the fifth (5ᵗʰ) strike. The sixth (6ᵗʰ) strike should be at your opponent's left knee. Your "**Abierta**" stance should also lower itself while you lower each "**Planchada**" strike at each level height. As you are executing these "**Planchada**" strikes, chamber your left-hand weapon on top of your right forearm. As you begin the strikes, initiate them from your left side with the cutting edges of your swords facing your opponent. The same is true from the left side as you are executing these **"Planchada"** strikes. Chamber your right-hand weapon on top of your left forearm. As you begin the strikes, initiate from your right side with the cutting edges of your swords facing your opponent. Once the first set of six (6) series of strikes are completed from the "abierta" stance as you are chambering your right-hand weapon on top of your left forearm, you will now swing **"Columpio"** your right foot back and pivot with your left foot into a "abierta" stance. While in the process of pivoting your feet from this "**Abierta**" stance, execute the Inward **"Planchada Abierta"** seventh (7th) strike with your right-hand weapon to your opponent's left knee and follow with a back hand **"Planchada Cerrada"** eighth (8th) strike with your left-hand weapon targeted about three (3) inches higher than the seventh (7th) strike. Follow with a back hand **"Planchada Cerrada"** ninth (9th) strike with your right-hand weapon to your opponent's right side. The target is about three (3) inches higher than the eighth (8th) strike. Now, pivot on the balls of your feet to the opposite side, your right foot at 3 o'clock, bending the right knee directly over the right toes with your left leg extended out, straight, at 9 o'clock, toes pointing forward 90 degrees, respective to the right foot. Again, while in the process of pivoting your feet from this "**Abierta**" stance, execute the Inward **"Planchada Abierta"** tenth (10th) strike with your left-hand weapon to your opponent's right leg about three (3) inches higher than the ninth (9th) strike. Follow with a back hand **"Planchada Cerrada"** eleventh (11th) strike with your right-hand weapon targeted about three (3) inches higher than the tenth (10th) strike. Then follow with a back hand **"Planchada Cerrada"** twelfth (12th) strike with your left-hand weapon to your opponent's left side targeted about three (3) inches higher than the previous eleventh (11th) strike. The twelfth (12th) strike should end at the height of your opponent's left mid-section. Your "**Abierta**" stance should also rise while you raise each "Planchada" strike at each level height. As you are executing these **"Planchada"** strikes, chamber your left-hand weapon on top of your right forearm. As you begin the strikes, initiate from your left side with the cutting edges of your swords facing your opponent. The same is true from the left side as you are executing these **"Planchada"** strikes. Chamber your right-hand weapon on top of your left forearm as you begin the strikes, initiating from your right side with the cutting edges of your swords facing your opponent. Once the series of twelve (12) strikes are completed from the "**Abierta**" stance, as you are chambering your right-hand weapon on top of your left forearm, you will now swing "Columpio" your right foot back and pivot with your left foot into a "**Abierta**" stance. This will end this series of "**Planchada**" strikes. Depending on the situation and the position of your opponent you can start these series of strikes at any height either descending or ascending. The "**Planchada Abierta**," "**Planchada Cerrada**," and "**Planchada Cerrada**" series of six descending strikes and six ascending strikes are based on the principle of Inward, Back Hand and Back Hand and is divided up into six (6) target strike areas, which is sometimes referred to Low, Low, Low, and Low, Low, Low or L, L, L, and L, L, L consisting of three (3) descending strikes per side. The same is true for the ascending strikes. They are also based on the principle of Inward, Back Hand and Back Hand and is divided up into six (6) target strike areas, sometimes called High, High, High, and High, High, High or H, H, H, and H, H, H consisting of three (3) ascending strikes per side.

Sombrada for "Planchada Escalera" Drill:

1. Execute a three (3) descending strike combination from the **"Abierta"** open body stance as described above. Starting with the right-hand weapon, execute an inward strike targeting your opponent's left mid-section and follow with your left-hand weapon, which is chambered on top of your right forearm. Execute a left-hand back hand strike targeting your opponent's left side but thee (3) inches lower than the previous strike. Now chambered on your left side in the closed strike position from after the first right hand strike, execute a right-hand back hand strike targeting your opponent's right leg but three (3) inches lower than your previous strike.

2. Pivot to the opposite side with your **"Abierta"** open body stance and execute a three (3) strike combination. Starting from the left side with the left-hand weapon, execute an inward strike targeting your opponent's right leg about three (3) inches lower than your previous strike. With your right-hand weapon, which is chambered on top of your left forearm, execute a right back hand strike targeting your opponent's right leg three (3) inches lower than your previous strike. Now chambered on your right side in the closed strike position from after the first left hand strike, execute a left back hand strike targeting your opponent's left knee.

3. Pivot to the opposite side and execute a three (3) ascending strike combination starting from the **"Abierta,"** open, body stance as described above. With the right-hand weapon, execute an inward strike targeting your opponent's left knee. Followed with your left-hand weapon, which is chambered on top of your right forearm, execute a left-hand back hand strike targeting your opponent's left leg but three (3) inches higher than the previous strike. Now chambered on your left side in the closed strike position from after the first right hand strike, execute a right-hand back hand strike targeting your opponent's right leg but three (3) inches higher than your previous strike.

4. Pivot to the opposite side and execute a three (3) strike combination. Starting from the left side with the left-hand weapon, execute an inward strike targeting your opponent's right leg about three (3) inches higher than your previous strike. With your right-hand weapon, which is chambered on top of your left forearm, execute a right back hand strike targeting your opponent's right leg three (3) higher than your previous strike. Now chambered on your right side in the closed strike position from after the first left hand strike, execute a left back hand strike targeting your opponent's left mid-section.

Note: while executing this Inward, Back Hand and Back Hand drill as you both strike at your target area, your weapons will hit each other forming an "X" at each height Low, Low and Low on each side and High, High and High on each side, or a series of six descending strikes and second series of six ascending strikes. This drill sequence can be repeated several times depending on the instructor.

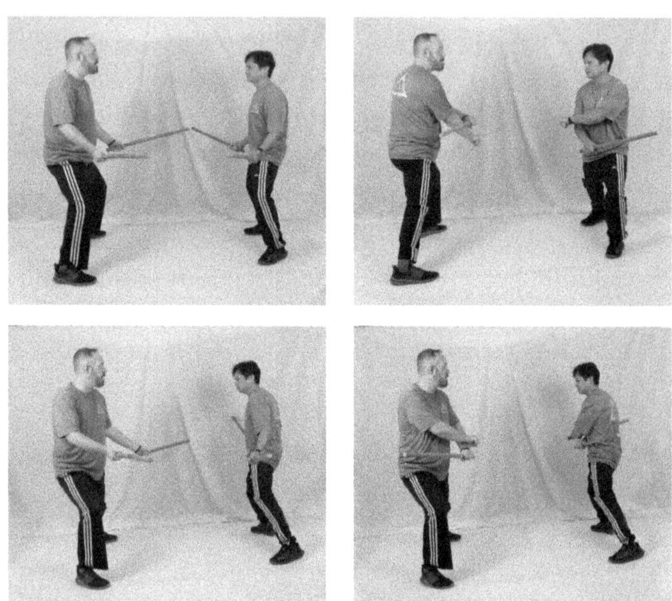

18. "Los Moros Redonda"

This Sinawali striking pattern combination means "The Moors whirlwind." It has a romantic Filipino reference as applied to Escrima to a reverse direction back hand **"Redonda"** circular strike as applied by the people in the southern Philippines commonly known and identified by the Spanish as the "Los Moros," or the Moors. They used two bladed weapons rotating in rapid secession, like a tornado, whirlwind, or cyclone. This technique is based on the principle of Back Hand, Back Hand Back, Back Hand. From a left foot lead, **"Laban Handa"** stance or **"Mandirigma"** stance with both of your weapons chambered at each side pointing upwards in a vertical position ready to parry, defend, or attack, step forward into a right foot lead stance and execute the Back Hand high strike by rotating your weapon in a clockwise "**Redonda**" circular motion with the right-hand weapon targeting your opponent's right temple, neck, or shoulder. As you are executing this back hand high strike and stepping forward with your right foot, chamber your left-hand weapon under your right armpit with the cutting edge of your sword facing your opponent. As you step forward, execute the first back hand high circular strike with your right-hand weapon. Immediately follow with a back hand high strike with the left-hand weapon that is chambered under the right arm pit. Strike your opponent's left temple, neck, or shoulder and follow with a back hand high strike with the right-hand weapon, which is now chambered on your left side near your left shoulder. The target area of this right back hand strike is to your opponent's right temple, neck, or shoulder. Once the first three (3) series of strikes are completed from the right foot lead stance, "**Redonda**" your right-hand weapon in a circular counterclockwise motion as you swing "**Columpio**" your right foot back and step forward with your left foot into a left foot lead stance. Execute the back hand high circular strike with the left-hand weapon targeting your opponent's left temple, neck, or shoulder. As you are executing this back hand high line circular strike and stepping forward with your left foot, chamber your right-hand weapon under your left armpit with the cutting edge of your sword facing your opponent. Immediately follow with a back hand high strike with the right-hand weapon that is chambered under the left arm pit to your opponent's right temple, neck, or shoulder. Follow with a back hand high strike with the left-hand weapon, which is now chambered on your right side near your right shoulder. The target area of this left back hand strike is to your opponent's left temple, neck, or shoulder. Once the second three (3) series of strikes are completed from the left foot lead stance, as you are chambering your left-hand weapon under your right armpit, you will now swing **"Columpio"** your left foot back and step forward with your right foot into a right foot lead stance completing the "**Los Moros Redonda**" or "**Moro Redonda**" series. The Six Back Hand High, Back Hand High and Back Hand High is divided up into three (3) target strike areas and is sometimes called High, High, High or H, H, H consisting of three (3) strikes per side.

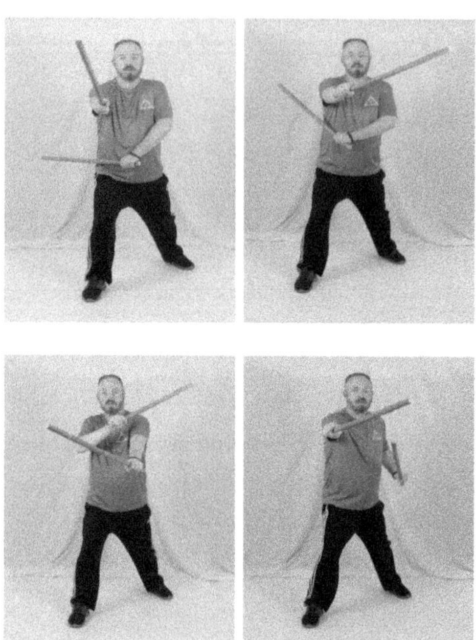

"Sombrada Los Moros Redonda" Drill

1. The right-hand weapon executes a three (3) strike combination. Starting from the right side with the right-hand weapon, execute a Back hand High clockwise circular strike targeting your opponent's right temple. With your left-hand weapon, which is chambered under your right arm pit, execute a left-hand back hand high strike targeting your opponent's left temple. Now chambered on your left side near your left shoulder, execute a right-hand back hand high strike targeting your opponent's right temple.

2. The left-hand weapon executes a three (3) strike combination. Starting from the left side with the left-hand weapon, execute a back hand counterclockwise high circular strike targeting your opponent's left temple. With your right-hand weapon, which is chambered under your left arm pit, execute a high right back hand strike targeting your opponent's right temple. Now chambered on your right side near your right shoulder,

execute a high left back hand strike targeting your opponent's left temple.

Note: while executing this high back hand circular strike, high back hand, and high back hand drill you both strike at your target area. Your weapons will hit each other forming an "X" at each height High, High, and High. It is necessary to adjust your height or lower your stance and weapon for each target area. This drill sequence can be repeated several times depending on the instructor and can be performed in a stationary manner in a **"De Fondo"** stance or in a **"Luton"** flowing foot work as you change into either a right foot lead or left foot lead stance while each time adjusting your rear leg and foot in a **"Columpio"** manner.

19. "Moro Redonda, Langit at Lupa"

This Sinawali striking pattern combination means "The Moors whirlwind with heaven and earth." It has a romantic Filipino reference as applied to Escrima to a reverse direction back hand **"Redonda"** circular strike, as applied by the people in the southern Philippines commonly known and identified by the Spanish as the "Los Moros," or the Moors. They used two bladed weapons rotating in rapid secession, like a tornado, whirlwind, or cyclone, with a combination of high and low strikes. It is very similar to the previous technique but now has added high and low strikes combinations. This technique is based on the principle of High Back Hand, Low Back Hand, High Back Hand. From a left foot lead, **"Laban Handa"** stance or **"Mandirigma"** stance, with both of your weapons chambered at each side pointing upwards in a vertical position ready to parry, defend, or attack, step forward into a right foot lead stance and execute the Back Hand high strike by rotating your weapon in a clockwise **"Redonda"** circular motion with the right-hand weapon targeting your opponent's right temple, neck, or shoulder. As you are executing this back hand high strike and stepping forward with your right foot, chamber your left-hand weapon under your right armpit with the cutting edge of your sword facing your opponent. Note: this action of stepping forward and chambering your left-hand weapon under your right armpit is in reality a parry, block or strike. Execute the first back hand high circular strike with your right-hand weapon. Follow with a back hand low strike with the left-hand weapon that is chambered under the right arm pit. Strike your opponent's left knee and immediately follow with a back hand high strike with the right-hand weapon, which is now chambered on your left side near your left shoulder. The target area of this right back hand strike is to your opponent's right temple, neck, or shoulder. Once the first three (3) series of strikes are completed from the right foot lead stance, **"Redonda"** your right-hand weapon in a circular counterclockwise motion as you swing **"Columpio"** your right foot back and step forward with your left foot into a left foot lead stance, execute the high back hand circular strike with the left-hand weapon, targeting your opponent's left temple, neck, or shoulder. As you are executing this back hand high line circular strike and stepping forward with your left foot, chamber your right-hand weapon under your left armpit with the cutting edge of your sword facing your opponent. Follow with a high back hand strike with the right-hand weapon that is chambered under the left arm pit to your opponent's right knee. Follow with a high back hand strike with the left-hand weapon, which is now chambered on your right side near your right shoulder. The target area of this left back hand strike is to your opponent's left temple, neck, or shoulder. Once the second three (3) series of strikes are completed from the left foot lead stance, as you are chambering your left-hand weapon under your right armpit, you will now swing **"Columpio"** your left foot back and step forward with your right foot into a right foot lead completing the **"Moro Redonda, Langit at Lupa"** series. The Six High Back Hand, Low Back

Hand, and High Back Hand is divided up into three (3) target strike areas and is sometimes called High, Low, High or H, L, H consisting of three (3) strikes per side.

Sombrada "Moro Redonda, Langit at Lupa" Drill

1. The right-hand weapon executes a three (3) strike combination. Starting from the right side with the right-hand weapon, execute a high back hand clockwise circular strike targeting your opponent's right temple. With your left-hand weapon, which is chambered under your right arm pit, execute a low left-hand back hand strike targeting your opponent's left knee. Now chambered on your left side near your left shoulder, execute a high right-hand back hand strike targeting your opponent's right temple.
2. The left-hand weapon executes a three (3) strike combination. Starting

from the left side with the left-hand weapon, execute a high back hand counterclockwise circular strike targeting your opponent's left temple. With your right-hand weapon, which is chambered under your left arm pit, execute a low right hand back hand strike targeting your opponent's right knee. Now chambered on your right side near your right shoulder, execute a high left hand back hand strike targeting your opponent's left temple.

Note: while executing this high back hand circular strike, high back hand, low Back hand drill as you both strike at your target area, your weapons will hit each other forming an "X" at each height High, Low and High. It is necessary to adjust your height or lower your stance and weapon for each target area. This drill sequence can be repeated several times, depending on the instructor, and can be performed in a stationary manner in, a "**De Fondo**" stance, or in a "**Luton**" flowing foot work as you change into either right foot lead or a left foot lead stance while each time adjusting your rear leg and foot in a "**Columpio**" manner.

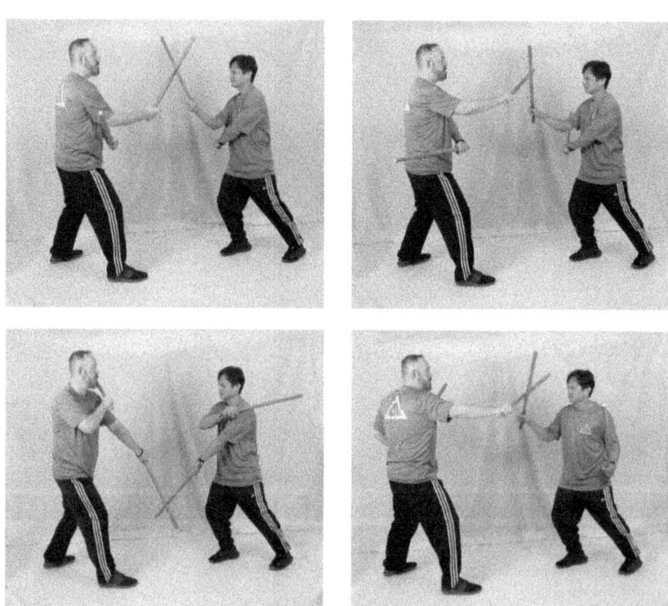

20. "De Cuerdas Redonda"

This Sinawali Striking Pattern is similar to the "**Moro Redonda**" Sinawali pattern technique, but this technique is now prefixed with an inward strike and immediately followed with the 'Los Moros Redonda"

Sinawali technique. This combination has four (4) strikes per side, or a total of eight (8) strikes. This technique means "Untie a cord or string with whirlwind." It has a romantic Filipino reference as applied to Escrima to rebound in rapid succession and deliver a reverse direction back hand "redonda" circular strike, like a tornado, whirlwind, or cyclone. This technique is based on the principle of inward, back hand reverse circular "**Redonda**" back hand, back hand, back hand. From a left foot lead, **"Laban Handa"** stance or **"Mandirigma"** stance, with both of your weapons chambered at each side pointing upwards in a vertical position ready to parry, defend, or attack, step forward into a right foot lead stance. Execute the Inward strike to your opponent's left temple, neck, or shoulder, and immediately as you strike your target, execute a high back hand strike by rotating your weapon in a clockwise "**Redonda**" circular motion with the right-hand weapon targeting your opponent's right temple, neck, right shoulder. As you are executing this high back hand strike and stepping forward with your right foot, chamber your left-hand weapon under your right armpit with the cutting edge of your sword facing your opponent. Now execute the inward strike to your opponent left temple, neck, or shoulder. Immediately "**Redonda**" a high back hand circular strike with your right-hand weapon to your opponent's right temple, neck, or shoulder, executing a high back hand strike with the left-hand weapon that is chambered under the right arm pit, and strike your opponent's left temple, neck, or shoulder. Immediately follow with a back hand high strike with the right-hand weapon, which is now chambered on your left side near your left shoulder. The target the area of this right back hand strike is to your opponent's right temple, neck, or shoulder. Once the first four (4) series of strikes are completed from the right foot lead stance, "**Redonda**" your left-hand weapon in a circular counterclockwise motion. As you swing **"Columpio"** your right foot back and step forward with your left foot into a left foot lead stance, execute the inward strike to your opponent's right temple, neck, or shoulder. Immediately strike your target, executing a high back hand strike by rotating your weapon in a counterclockwise "**Redonda**" circular motion with the left-hand weapon targeting your opponent's left temple, neck, or shoulder. As you are executing this back hand high strike and stepping forward with your left foot, chamber your right-hand weapon under your left armpit with the cutting edge of your sword facing your opponent. Immediately follow with a high back hand strike with the right-hand weapon that is chambered under the left arm pit to your opponent's right temple, neck, or shoulder. Follow with a high back hand strike with the left-hand weapon, which is now chambered on your right side near your right shoulder. The target area of this left back hand strike is to your opponent's left temple, neck, or shoulder. Once the second four (4) series of strikes are completed from the left foot lead stance, as you are chambering your left-hand weapon under your right armpit, you will now swing **"Columpio"** your left foot back and step forward into a right foot lead stance completing the **"De Cuerdas Redonda"** series. The eight Inward, **"Redonda"** Back Hand High, Back Hand High and Back Hand High is divided up into four (4) target strikes areas and is sometimes called High, High, High, High or H, H, H, H consisting of four (4) strikes per side.

21. "De Cuerdas Redonda, Langit at Lupa"

This Sinawali striking pattern is very similar to the "**De Cuerdas Redonda**" Sinawali pattern technique but this technique now has high and low strike combinations. This combination has four (4) strikes per side or a total of eight (8) strikes. This technique means "Untie a cord or string with whirlwind heaven and earth" but has a romantic Filipino reference as applied to Escrima to rebound in rapid succession and deliver a reverse direction back hand "redonda" circular, like a tornado, whirlwind, or cyclone, with high and low strike combinations. This technique is based on the principle of Inward High, Back Hand High reverse circular "**Redonda**," Back Hand Back Low, Back Hand High. From a left foot lead **"Laban Handa"** stance or **"Mandirigma"** stance with both of your weapons chambered at each side pointing upwards in a vertical position ready to parry, defend or attack, step forward into a right foot lead stance and execute the inward strike to your opponent's left temple, neck or left shoulder. Immediately as you strike your target, execute a high back hand strike by rotating your weapon in a clockwise "**Redonda**" circular motion with the right-hand weapon, targeting your opponent's right temple, neck or right shoulder. As you are executing this back hand high strike and stepping forward with your right foot, chamber your left-hand weapon under your right armpit with the cutting edge of your sword facing your opponent. As you execute the inward strike to your opponent left temple, neck, or left shoulder and immediately "**Redonda**" a back hand high circular strike with your right-hand weapon to your opponent's right temple, neck, or right shoulder. Execute a low back hand strike with the left-hand weapon, which is chambered under the right arm pit, and strike your opponent's left knee. Immediately follow with a high back hand strike with the right-hand weapon, which is now chambered on your left side near your left shoulder. The target area of this right back hand strike is to your opponent's right temple, neck, or right shoulder. Once the first four (4) series of strikes are completed from the right foot lead stance, "**Redonda**" your left-hand weapon in a circular counterclockwise motion as you swing **"Columpio"** your right foot back and step forward with your left foot into a left foot lead stance. Execute an inward strike to your opponent's right temple, neck, or shoulder, and immediately as you strike your target, execute a high back hand strike by rotating your weapon in a counterclockwise "**Redonda**" circular motion with the left-hand weapon, targeting your opponent's left temple, neck, or shoulder. As you are executing this back hand high strike and stepping forward with your left foot, chamber your right-hand weapon under your left armpit with the cutting edge of your sword facing your opponent. Immediately follow with a high back hand strike with the right-hand weapon, which is chambered under the left arm pit, to your opponent's right knee. Follow with a high back hand strike with the left-hand weapon, which is now chambered on your right side near your right shoulder, targeting your left back hand strike to your opponent's left temple, neck, or shoulder. Once the second four (4) series of strikes is completed from the left foot lead stance, chamber your left-hand weapon under your right armpit. You will now swing **"Columpio"** your left foot back and step forward into a right foot lead stance completing the "**De Cuerdas Redonda, Langit at Lupa**" series. The eight (8) Inward, "**Redonda**" high back hand, low back hand, and high back hand is divided up into four (4) target strikes areas and is sometimes called High, High, Low, High or H, H, L, H consisting of four (4) strikes per side.

Sombrada for the "De Cuerdas Redonda, Langit at Lupa" Drill

1. The right-hand weapon executes a four (4) strike combination. Starting from the right side, with the right-hand weapon, execute an inward strike to your opponent's left temple and follow with a high back hand clockwise circular strike, targeting your opponent's right temple. With your left-hand weapon, which is chambered under your right arm pit, execute a low left-hand back hand target to your opponent's left knee. Now chambered on your left side near your left shoulder, execute a right-hand high back hand strike targeting your opponent's right temple.

2. The left-hand weapon executes a four (4) strike combination. Starting from the left side with the left-hand weapon, execute an inward strike to your opponent's right temple and follow with a back hand counterclockwise high circular strike, targeting your opponent's left temple. With your right-hand weapon, which is chambered under your left arm pit, execute a low right-hand back hand strike, targeting your opponent's right knee. Now chambered on your right side near your right shoulder, execute a high left-hand back hand strike targeting your opponent's left temple.

Note: While executing this high inward, high back hand circular, low back hand, and high back hand drill you both target one another's target area. Your weapons will hit each other forming an "X" at each height Inward High, High, Low and High. This drill sequence can be repeated several times, depending on the instructor, and can be performed in a stationary manner in a "**De Fondo**" stance or in a "**Luton**" flowing foot work as you change into either right foot or a left foot lead stance while each time adjusting your rear leg and foot in a "**Columpio**" manner.

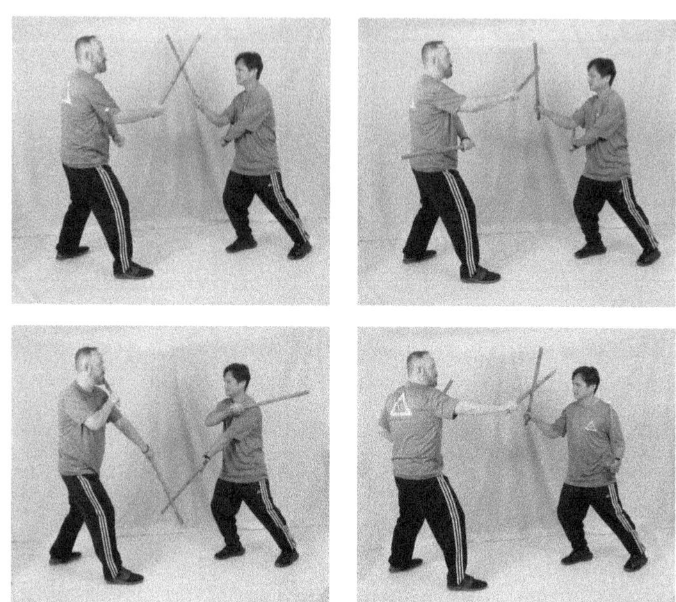

22. "La Cometa, Redonda, Salot Saboy"

This technique is a ten (10) multiple Striking Pattern and means the "The comet with reverse upward direction whirlwind" but the true meaning or the romantic Filipino reference as applied to Escrima is "like the speed of a comet rotating in circular motion and from the reverse vortex whirlwind, like a tornado as it sucks up your opponent into devastation with a combination of inward and continuous upward strikes." This technique is based on the principle of Inward High, Back Hand Low, Inward Hand Low, Back Hand Low and Back Hand Low per each side. From a left foot lead **"Laban Handa"** stance or **"Mandirigma"** stance with both of your weapons chambered at each side with your weapons pointing upwards in a vertical position ready to parry, defend, or attack, step forward into a right foot lead stance, and execute the high inward strike, starting with the right-hand weapon targeting your opponent's left temple. As you are executing this high inward strike and stepping forward with your right foot, chamber your left wrist on top of your right forearm in the valley of your right elbow with the cutting edge of your sword facing your opponent. Note: this action of stepping forward and chambering your left-hand weapon on top of your right forearm is in reality a parry, block, or strike. Again, you do not simply chamber your left-hand weapon on top your right forearm because it will completely expose your left side for a counter strike. Now, execute the first inward high line strike with your right-hand weapon to your opponent's left temple. Then immediately pivot on the balls of your feet into a **"Mandirigma"** stance as you scoop your right-hand weapon downward in a counterclockwise motion and deliver a back hand low **"Aldabis"** strike to your opponent's right knee, simultaneously delivering a high inward **"Planchada"** strike to your opponent's right temple, neck, or right shoulder. Once this is completed, you should be in the classic **"Mandirigma"** warrior's back stance with your right-hand weapon pointing downward and in the same angle of your right leg, now extended out straight. Your left-hand weapon is now chambered on your left side with your weapon pointing upward in a vertical position. Now step forward into a left foot lead stance and execute the low inward **"Saboy"** strike starting with the left-hand weapon, targeting your opponent's right knee. As you are executing this inward low line **"Saboy"** strike and stepping forward with your left foot, chamber your right-hand weapon on top of your left forearm with the cutting edge of your sword facing your opponent. Then execute the first inward low line **"Saboy"** strike with your left-hand weapon to your opponent's right knee. Immediately follow with a back hand low **"Aldabis"** strike with the right-hand weapon that is chambered on top of the left forearm to your opponent's right knee. Immediately follow with a back hand low **"Aldabis"** strike from the left-hand weapon to your opponent's left knee or lower open target. While you are executing this second **"Aldabis"** strike, chamber your right-hand weapon into a Roof Block position directly over your head. As you rotate your weapon counterclockwise to this position, pivot on the balls of your feet into a classic "Mandirigma" warrior's back stance with your left-hand weapon pointing downward and in the same angle of your left leg now extended out, straight. Your right-hand weapon now chambered over your head in a **"Sinalakot"** position. This should complete the first series of strikes starting from the right side. From this classic **"Mandirigma"** warrior's back stance, simultaneously pivot on the balls of your feet into a left foot lead stance. While executing this stance change, **"Redonda"** your left-hand weapon up and around your head in a clockwise circular motion and deliver to your opponent's right temple an inward "**Redonda**" strike. As you execute a counterclockwise "**Redonda**" strike to your opponent's left temple, neck, or shoulder with your right hand weapon from the **"Sinalakot"** position, strike through and stop your right hand weapon in the valley of your left hand inside elbow. Immediately pivot on the balls of your feet into a **"Mandirigma"** stance as you scoop your left-hand weapon downward in a clockwise motion and deliver a back hand low "**Aldabis**" strike to your opponent's right knee. Simultaneously, deliver a high inward "**Planchada**" strike to your opponent's left temple, neck, or shoulder. Once this is completed, you should be in the classic "**Mandirigma**" warrior's back stance with your left-hand weapon pointing downward and in the same angle of your left leg now extended out, straight. Your right-hand weapon is now chambered on your right side with your weapon pointing upward in a vertical position and your right leg bent. Now step forward into a right-foot lead stance and execute the inward low **"Saboy"** strike starting with the right-hand weapon, targeting your opponent's left knee. As you are executing this inward low line **"Saboy"** strike and stepping forward with your right foot, chamber your left-hand weapon on top of your right forearm with the cutting edge of your sword facing your opponent. Execute the first inward low line **"Saboy"** strike with your right-hand weapon to your opponent's left knee. Immediately follow with a back hand low **"Aldabis"** strike with the left-hand weapon that is chambered on top of the right forearm to your opponent's left knee. Follow with a back hand low **"Aldabis"** strike from the left-hand weapon to your opponent's right knee or lower open target. While you are executing this second "**Aldabis**" strike, chamber your left-hand weapon into a **"Sinalakot"** position directly over your head. As you rotate your weapon clockwise to this position, pivot on the balls of your feet into a classic "**Mandirigma**" warrior's back stance with your right-hand weapon pointing downward and in the same angle of your right leg now extended out, straight. Your left-hand weapon is now chambered over your head in a **"Sinalakot"** position with your left leg bent. This should complete the second series of strikes starting from the left side. The "**La Cometa, Redonda, Salot Saboy**" Ten combination strikes of Inward High, Back Hand Low, Inward Hand Low, Back Hand Low and Back Hand Low is divided up into five (5) target combination strike areas and is sometimes called High, Low, Low, Low, Low or H, L, L, L, L, consisting of five (5) strikes per side of "**Taga**", "**Aldabis**", "**Saboy**", "**Aldabis**", "**Aldabis**," but with double striking combinations of "**Planchada**" strikes as you transition or prefix from side to side.

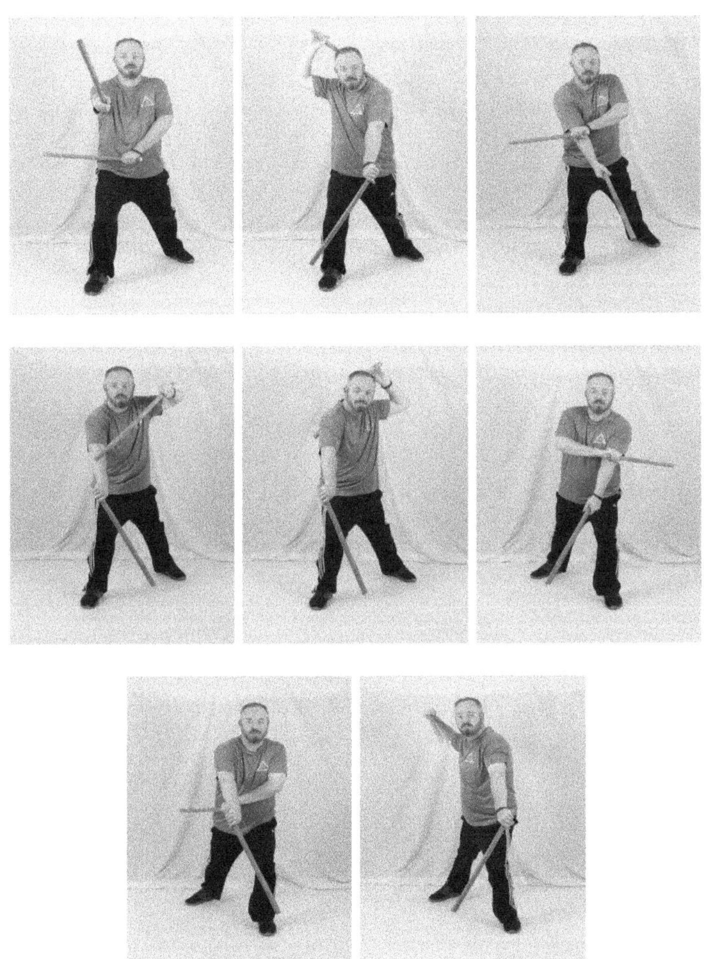

Sombrada for "La Cometa, Redonda, Salot Saboy"

1. The right-hand weapon executes a five (5) strike combination. Starting from the right side with the right-hand weapon, execute a high inward strike targeting your opponent's left temple, as you execute a inward strike to your opponent's right temple, neck, or shoulder and follow through and stops inside the valley of your right hand elbow with your left wrist cradled in the valley of your right inside elbow. Pivot into a "**Mandirigma**" stance as you "**Aldabis**" low with your left-hand weapon and "**Planchada**" high with your right-hand weapon. Then step forward into a left foot lead stance and execute an inward "**Saboy**" strike to your opponent's right knee. Now chambered on your left forearm execute a "**Aldabis**" strike to your opponent's right knee. As you start to deliver you left-hand weapon for a "**Aldabis**" strike to your opponent's left knee or any open lower target, pivot into a "**Mandirigma**" stance position and chamber your right-hand weapon into a "**Sinalakot**" position.

2. The left-hand weapon executes a five (5) strike combination. Starting from the left side with the left-hand weapon, execute a high inward strike targeting your opponent's right temple as you execute an inward strike to your opponent's left temple, neck, left shoulder. Follow through and stop inside the valley of your left-hand elbow with your right wrist cradled in the valley of your left inside elbow. Then pivot into a "**Mandirigma**" stance as you "**Aldabis**" low with your right-hand weapon and "**Planchada**" high with your left-hand weapon. Then step forward into a right foot lead stance and execute an inward "**Saboy**" strike to your opponent's left knee. Now chambered on your right forearm execute an "**Aldabis**" strike to your opponent's left knee. As you start to deliver the right-hand weapon for an "**Aldabis**" to your opponent's right knee or any open lower target, pivot into a "**Mandirigma**" stance position and chamber your left-hand weapon into a "**Sinalakot**" position.

Note: while executing this Inward Low, Back Hand Low, Inward Low, Back hand Low and Back Hand Low drill as you both target each other's target area, your weapons will hit each other forming an "X" at each height High, Low, Low, Low, Low. This drill sequence can be repeated several times depending on the instructor.

23. "Magbabayo Redonda, Aldabis sa Ilalim"

This Lakbay Sinawali technique is based on the principle of downward figure eight which is a High Inward, High Back Hand, "**Redonda**", High Inward, High Back Hand, High Back Hand, "**Abanico**", and upward "**Aldabis**" strike up through the centerline. This technique has a Filipino romantic expression for eight (8) striking weaving combinations per each side that incorporates faking or drawing your opponent into this deadly striking pattern. It is in reality a prefix and suffix striking combination consisting of Heaven Six or Heaven and Earth Six and is commonly known within the circles of Escrima/Kali as the "Villabrille Eight (8)" or "Villabrille Sixteen (16)" depending on whom you are talking to or are associated with in an Escrima/Kali organization. From a left foot lead **"Laban Handa"** stance or **"Mandirigma"** stance, with both of your weapons chambered at each side pointing upwards in a vertical position ready to parry, defend, or attack, step forward into a right foot lead stance and execute the Inward downward figure eight (8), or **"Magbabayo"** strike, starting with the right-hand weapon targeting your opponent's left temple, neck, or shoulder. The returning back hand strike targets your opponent's right temple, neck, or shoulder. As you are executing this inward high line strike and stepping forward with your right foot, chamber your left-hand weapon under your right armpit with the cutting edge of your sword facing your opponent. You then step into the chamber after a left-hand weapon parry, block, or strike, and you execute the first inward high line strike with your right-hand weapon. Immediately after the **"Magbabayo"** strike is executed, **"Redonda"** your right-hand weapon around your head counterclockwise. As you are rotating your weapon, follow with a high back hand snap strike with the left-hand weapon, which is chambered under the right arm pit, with the same target area of the first strike. After this back hand strike, immediately chamber back to the same chambered position under your right armpit. Now from the rotating right-hand weapon going around your head in a counterclockwise circular "redonda" motion, execute the same strike targeting the same area as before which is your opponent's left temple, neck, or shoulder. Again, execute the left-hand back hand with the left-hand weapon, which is now chambered under your right armpit, and strike your opponent's right temple, neck, or shoulder. After this strike, your right-hand weapon should now be chambered near your left shoulder. Now execute a back hand strike to your opponent's right temple, neck, or shoulder and **"Abanico"** counterclockwise to strike your opponent's left temple, neck, or shoulder. Then, lower your right-hand weapon down to almost near the ground or floor at centerline and execute an **"Aldabis sa Ilalim"** strike up through centerline of your opponent's body, exiting through the right side of your opponent's neck. This series of eight (8) strikes is completed from the right foot lead stance. As you are chambering your right-hand weapon under your left armpit, you will now swing **"Columpio"** your right back and step forward with your left foot into a left foot lead stance and execute the inward downward figure eight (8), or **"Magbabayo"** strike, starting with the left-hand weapon, targeting your opponent's right temple, neck or right shoulder. The returning back hand target is to your opponent's left temple, neck or left shoulder, as you are executing this inward high line strike and stepping forward with your left foot. Chamber your right-hand weapon under your left armpit with the cutting edge of your sword facing your opponent. Note: this action of stepping forward and chambering your right-hand weapon under your left armpit is in reality a parry, block, or strike. Immediately after the **"Magbabayo"** strike is executed, **"Redonda"** your left-hand weapon strike around your head clockwise. As you are rotating your weapon, follow with a high back hand snap strike with the right-hand weapon that is chambered under the left arm pit to the same target area of the first strike. After this back hand strike, immediately chamber back to the same chambered position, under your left armpit. Now from the rotating left-hand weapon going around your head in a clockwise circular **"Redonda"** motion, execute the strike to the same target area as before, which is your opponent's right temple, neck, or shoulder. Again, execute the back hand strike with the right-hand weapon, which is now chambered on your left armpit, striking your opponent's right temple, neck, or shoulder. After this strike, your left-hand weapon should now be chambered near your right shoulder. Now execute a back hand strike to your opponent's left temple, neck, or shoulder and **"Abanico"** clockwise to strike your opponent's right temple, neck, or shoulder. Then, lower your left-hand weapon down near the ground or floor at centerline and execute an **"Aldabis sa Ilalim"** strike up through the centerline of your opponent's body, existing through the left side of your opponent's neck. This series of eight (8) series of strikes are completed from the left foot lead stance. As you are chambering your right-hand weapon under your left armpit, you will now swing **"Columpio"** your right foot back and step forward with your left foot into a left foot lead stance, completing the series of strikes from the right and left sides.

Notes:
1. This technique is performed differently when using a stick as a weapon instead of a steel fabricated sword. The back hand snap hit high or low before the "redonda" strike is usually eliminated when using a stick as a weapon and the centerline drop is usually counted as it strikes the

floor for the seventh 7th strike. But in a bladed application, you never drop or bounce your sword off the ground. Steel swords are tempered and bouncing one end of it against the ground or floor can cause small minute cracks and in time could eventually crack through and break off. Also, a bladed weapon in the Philippines is regarded as a sacred item, instrument, or weapon and is usually treated with respect. A practitioner of the art of Escrima/Kali lives by the principles of Escrima/Kali as it is represented by the Kali triangle which is Love, Compassion and Humility. This is usually always inculcated by the instructor or teacher either directly or indirectly by his or her examples and character during a training session.

2. This technique can be performed by using the "Heaven and Earth Six" sinawali pattern of High, Low, High as you prefix and suffix this sinawali striking combination for an eight (8) count per side.

3. There are many versions of this commonly known "Villabrille Eight (8)" this is only one (1) of many versions practiced within the Escrima/Kali community of Filipino Martial Artists. This technique is really called "**Magbabayo Redonda, Aldabis sa Ilalim**" and has several versions or variations of it, but in this book only one is shown and some variations are prefixed and suffixed with additional techniques that can have as much as twelve strike per side. "**Magbabayo Redonda, Aldabis sa Ilalim**" Eight (8) count Inward High, Back Hand High, Snap Back Hand High, Redonda, Inward High, Back Hand High, Back Hand High, Abanico and Aldabis is divided up into eight (8) target strike areas and is sometimes called High, High, High, High, High, High, High, High or H, H, H, H, H, H, H, H consisting of eight (8) strikes per side.

Sombrada for "Magbabayo Redonda, Aldabis sa Ilalim" Drill

1. The right-hand weapon executes an eight (8) strike combination. Starting from the right side with the right-hand weapon, execute an inward high target to your opponent's left temple and strike through as you "Magbabayo," or downward figure eight (8), and return and strike your opponent's right temple. Then "redonda" around your head counterclockwise, and as you are in the process of rotating your "Redonda" around your head with your left-hand weapon, which is chambered under your right arm pit, execute a left-hand snap back hand high target to your opponent's left temple. Immediately it chambers back to the original chambered position under your right armpit. Immediately follow with the "Redonda" strike to your opponent's left temple and strike through. Chamber your right-hand weapon on your left side in the No. 2 "Bartical" strike position and execute a left-hand back hand high target to your opponent's left temple. Immediately follow with a right-hand back hand strike to your opponent's right temple. Then "Abanico" the right-hand weapon to the opposite side and strike your opponent's left temple. Drop your weapon down near the floor at centerline of your opponent and execute a "Aldabis sa Ilalim" slash upward through the centerline of your opponent and out through the right side of your opponent's neck. Note: dropping of your weapon down centerline is in reality a "Bagsak" downward slash cut against your opponent's centerline.

2. The left-hand weapon executes an eight (8) strike combination. Starting

from the left side with the left-hand weapon, execute an inward high target to your opponent's right temple and strike through as you "Magbabayo," or downward figure eight (8), and return, striking your opponent's left temple. Then "redonda" around your head clockwise, and as you are in the process of rotating your "Redonda" around your head with your right-hand weapon, which is chambered under your left arm pit, execute a right-hand snap back hand high target to your opponent's right temple. Immediately it chambers back to the original chambered position under your left armpit. Immediately follow with the "Redonda" strike to your opponent's right temple and strike through and chamber your left-hand weapon on your right side in the No. 2 "Bartical" strike position. Execute a right-hand back hand high target to your opponent's right temple. Immediately follow with a left-hand back hand strike to your opponent's left temple. Then "Abanico" the left-hand weapon to the opposite side and strike your opponent's right temple and drop your weapon down to near the floor at centerline of your opponent, executing a "Aldabis sa Ilalim" slash upward through the centerline of your opponent and out through the left side of your opponent's neck. Note: dropping of your weapon down centerline is in reality a "Bagsak" downward slash cut against your opponent's centerline.

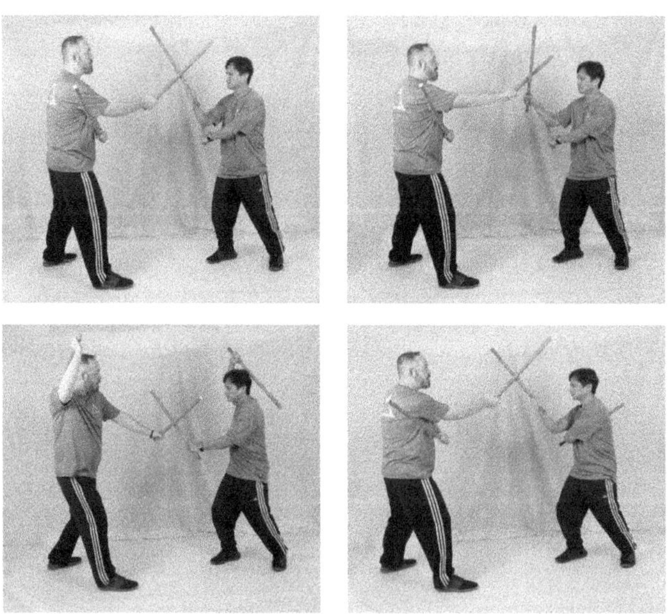

24. "Combate General"

This technique is based on the principle of fighting your opponent in four (4) quarters positions consisting of four (4) coordinate stations at 90 degrees of each other for each station or segment. For those who train using a clock system, imagine your opponent is at 12 o'clock and you are facing your opponent, stationed at 6 o'clock. Once the sinawali technique is completed at this station from 12 o'clock and 6 o'clock, you and your opponent will move clockwise 90 degrees respective of each other - your opponent will move to 3 o'clock, and you will move to 9 o'clock. Once the sinawali technique is completed at this station or segment, you and your opponent will move clockwise 90 degrees respective of each other - your opponent will move to 6 o'clock, and you will move to 12 o'clock. Again, once the sinawali technique is completed at this station or segment, you and your opponent will move clockwise 90 degrees respective of each other - your opponent will move to 9 o'clock, and you will move to 3 o'clock. Again, once the sinawali technique is completed at this station or segment, you and your opponent will move clockwise 90 degrees respective of each other - your opponent will move to 12 o'clock, and you will move to 6 o'clock, or back to the original position or station. Now that you have completed sinawali technique back at the original position, you and your opponent will move 90 degrees counterclockwise respective of each other - your opponent will move to 9 o'clock, and you will move to 3 o'clock. Again, once the sinawali technique is completed at this station or segment, you and your opponent will move counterclockwise 90 degrees respective of each other - your opponent will move to 6 o'clock, and you will move to 12 o'clock. Here again when the sinawali technique is completed at this station or segment, you and your opponent will move counterclockwise 90 degrees respective of each other - your opponent will move to 3 o'clock, and you will move to 9 o'clock. Once the sinawali technique is completed at this station or segment, you and your opponent will move counterclockwise 90 degrees respective of each other - your opponent will move to 12 o'clock, and you will move to 6 o'clock, or back to the original position or station. This will complete one rotation, each traveling counterclockwise and clockwise around your opponent. This technique is called "**Combate General**" and is based on the style of Escrima known as "Estilo de Salon," or a dancing style of moving and continuously adjusting your footwork rhythmically as if you were dancing while pivoting and swinging using the female triangle of footwork at each station or segment. Note: this style or technique of footwork only works on even terrain, in tournament play, or when you have multiple opponents. However, as stated before, it is not suited or recommended for uneven ground or slippery terrain. While in a left foot lead **"Laban Handa"** stance or

"Mandirigma" stance with both of your weapons chambered at each side with your weapons pointing upwards in a vertical position ready to parry, defend or attack, step forward into a right foot lead stance. Execute the inward high strike, starting with the right-hand weapon, targeting your opponent's left temple, neck, or left shoulder. As you are executing this inward high line strike and stepping forward with your right foot, chamber your left-hand weapon under your right armpit with the cutting edge of your sword facing your opponent. Note: this action of stepping forward and chambering your left-hand weapon under your right armpit is in reality a parry, block, or strike. The reason you do not simply chamber your left-hand weapon under your right armpit is because it will completely expose your left side for a counter strike. Then immediately follow with a back hand high strike with the left-hand weapon that is chambered under the right arm pit to the same target area of the first strike. Immediately follow with a back hand high strike with the right-hand weapon, which is now chambered on your left side near your left shoulder. The target area of this right back hand strike is to your opponent's right temple, neck, or shoulder. Once the first three (3) series of strikes are completed from the right foot lead stance, as you are chambering your right-hand weapon under your left armpit, you will now swing **"Columpio"** your right foot back and step forward with your left foot into a left foot lead stance. Note: the continuous swing **"Columpio"** action of rhythmically swinging and adjusting your feet or foot work into a different stance from one side to the other side is sometimes called **"Luton"** in Tagalog and **"Flujo"** in Chabacano or Spanish and means "flow." It has a Filipino romantic meaning of rhythmically flowing as if one is dancing to a given tempo, like in the dancing style of Escrima known as "Estilo de Salon." Now that you are in a left foot lead stance, execute the inward high strike, starting with the left-hand weapon, targeting your opponent's right temple, neck, or shoulder. As you are executing this inward high line strike and stepping forward with your right foot, chamber your right-hand weapon under your left armpit with the cutting edge of your sword facing your opponent. Then immediately follow with a back hand high strike with the right-hand weapon, which is chambered under the left arm pit, to the same target area of the first strike and immediately followed with a back hand high strike with the left-hand weapon, which is now chambered on your right side near your right shoulder. The target area of this left back hand strike is to your opponent's left temple, neck, or shoulder. Once the second three (3) series of strikes are completed from the left foot lead stance, you will chamber your left-hand weapon under your right armpit and swing **"Columpio"** your left foot back and step forward with your right foot into a right foot lead stance, completing the Heaven Six strike series. The Heaven Six Inward High, Back Hand High and Back Hand High is divided up into three (3) target strike areas and is sometimes called High, High, High or H, H, H consisting of three (3) strikes per side.

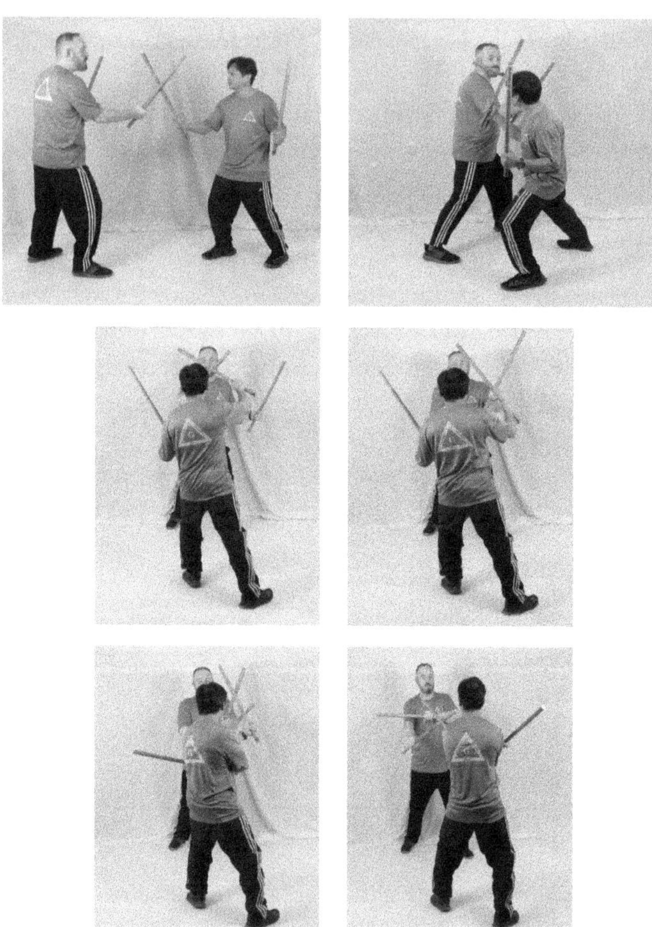

25. "Metamorphosis"

This technique romantically refers to a butterfly emerging from its cocoon. This twelve (12) strike combination combines the 7th and 9th techniques, Ceilo Seis and Salot Saboy. While in a left foot lead, **"Laban Handa"** stance or **"Mandirigma"** stance, with both of your weapons chambered at each side pointing upwards in a vertical position ready to parry, defend, or attack, step forward into a right foot lead stance and swing **"Columpio"** your left foot to directly behind your right foot lead stance. Execute the inward high strike, starting with the right-hand weapon. Stepping forward with your right foot, chamber your left-hand weapon under your right armpit with the cutting edge of your sword facing your opponent. Note: this action of stepping forward and chambering your left-hand weapon under your right armpit is in reality a parry, block or strike. The reason you do not simply chamber your left-hand weapon under your right armpit is because it will completely expose your left side for a counter strike. Then immediately follow with a back hand high strike with the left-hand weapon that is chambered under the right arm pit. It is the same target area of the first strike and immediately followed with a back hand high strike with the right-hand weapon, which is now chambered on your left side, near your left shoulder. The target area of this right back hand strike is to your opponent's right temple, neck, or shoulder. Once the first three (3) series of strikes are completed from the right foot lead stance, you are chambering your right-hand weapon on top of your left forearm. You will now swing **"Columpio"** your right foot back and step forward with your left foot into a left foot lead stance with 60% of your weight on your forward left foot lead stance. Now, execute the inward low **"Saboy"** strike, starting with the left-hand weapon, targeting your opponent's right knee. As you are executing this inward low line **"Saboy"** strike and stepping forward with your left foot, chamber your right-hand weapon over on top of your left forearm with the cutting edge of your sword facing your opponent. Immediately follow with a back hand low **"Aldabis"** strike with the right-hand weapon that is chambered on top of the left forearm to your opponent's right knee and follow with a back hand low "**Aldabis**" strike with the left-hand weapon to your opponent's left knee. Once the second third (3rd) series of **"Saboy"**, **"Aldabis"**, **"Aldabis"** strikes are completed from the left foot lead stance, chamber your left-hand weapon on top of your right forearm. You will now swing, **"Columpio,"** your left foot back and step forward with your right foot into a right foot lead stance and execute the inward low **"Saboy"** strike, starting with the right-hand weapon, targeting your opponent's left knee. As you are executing this inward low line strike and stepping forward with your right foot, chamber your left-hand weapon over on top of your right forearm with the cutting edge of your sword facing your opponent. As you execute the first inward low line **"Saboy"** strike with your right-hand weapon to your opponent's left knee, immediately follow with a back hand low **"Aldabis"** strike with the left-hand weapon that is chambered on top of the right forearm to your opponent's left knee. Immediately follow with a back hand low "**Aldabis**" strike with the right-hand weapon to your opponent's right knee. The third three (3) series of strikes are completed from the right foot lead stance as you are chambering your right-hand weapon over on top of your left forearm. You will now swing **"Columpio"** your right foot back and step forward with your left foot into a left foot lead stance with 60% of your weight on your forward left foot lead stance. Now that you are in a left foot lead stance, execute the inward high strike starting with the left-hand weapon. The target is to your opponent's right temple, neck, or shoulder as you are executing this inward high line strike. Stepping forward with your right foot, chamber your right-hand weapon under your left armpit with the cutting edge of your sword facing your opponent. Immediately follow with a back hand high strike with the right-hand weapon that is chambered under the left arm pit to the same target area of the first strike. This is immediately followed with a back hand high strike with the left-hand weapon, which is now chambered on your right side, near your right shoulder. The target area of this left back hand strike is to your opponent's left temple, neck, or left shoulder. Once the fourth three (3) series of strikes are completed from the left foot lead stance, chamber your left-hand weapon under your right armpit. You will now swing, **"Columpio,"** your left foot back and step forward with your right foot into a right foot lead stance, completing the Metamorphosis strike series.

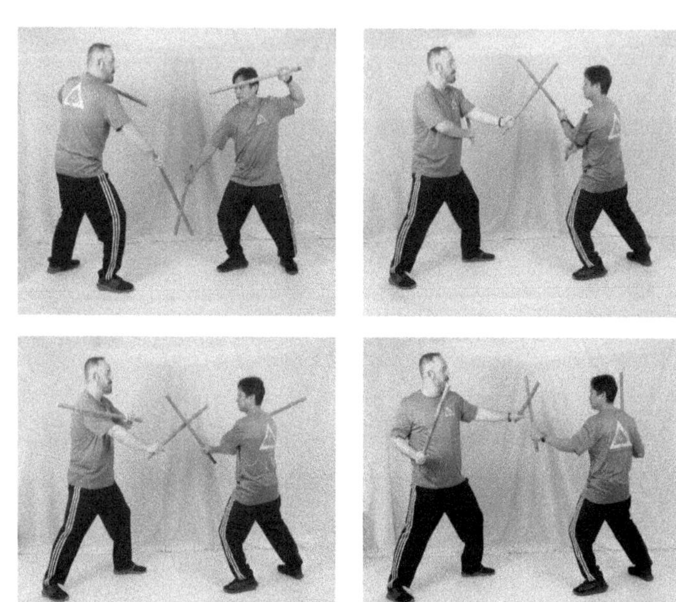

CHAPTER EIGHT

The Ten Line Drills

The ten (10) line drills described below are from what I remember my father and Mr. Hipolito practicing in the backyard when I was a child. More line drills can be derived from the 25 techniques described in Chapter Six by utilizing the prefixing and suffixing method to augment techniques and link them together. Every practitioner of Escrima should explore and work to make the art their own through their own expression of the techniques they learn. These line drills are good for learning how the techniques and principles of Galleon Clan Escrima work together providing an effective and diverse weapon-based fighting system.

The first 6-line drills are designed for learning the mechanics of footwork and body placement by having the two training partners performing the same techniques, mirroring each other throughout the line drill until the disarms at the end of each line drill. Line drill 1 introduces basic techniques and structure with each line drill after it introduces new and different concepts through more advanced techniques.

The last 4-line drills, 7-10, introduce you fighting against an uncooperative opponent. Both training partners will be performing different techniques simultaneously. These last 4-line drills introduce single weapon vs double weapon fighting. This is introduced for there may be a time where you lose a weapon in battle or must battle with only one weapon when your opponent has two weapons.

<h1 style="text-align:center">Line Drill #1</h1>

1. Kop-Kop High & Kop-Kop Low in right foot lead
2. Kop-Kop High & Kop-Kop Low in left foot lead
3. Abecedario "High, Low, High" in right foot lead
4. Abecedario "High, Low, High" in left foot lead
5. Heaven Six in right foot and left foot leads
6. Heaven Six in right and left foot leads
7. Heaven & Earth Six in right & then left foot lead
8. Heaven & Earth Six in right & then left foot lead
9. Heaven Six in right & then left foot lead
10. No.1 Strike Cadena Real in right foot lead
11. Combate General Clockwise Cadena Real & Prefix Heaven Six in right & left foot lead
12. Combate General Counterclockwise Cadena Real & Prefix Heaven Six in left & right foot lead
13. Magbabayo Redonda, Aldabis sa Ilalim in right & then left foot lead
14. Heaven Six in right foot then left foot lead
15. Inside "Vine" Disarm Against No.1 "Taga" Strike in right foot lead
16. "Hook" Disarm Against No.2 "Bartical" Strike in right foot lead
17. Heaven Six in right foot lead
18. Avalanche Doble in right foot lead

LINE DRILL #2

1. Kop-Kop High & Kop-Kop Low in right foot lead
2. Kop-Kop High & Kop-Kop Low in left foot lead
3. Prefix Abecedario High, Low, High in right foot
4. Prefix Abecedario High, Low, High in left foot lead
5. Moro-Moro Heaven Six Strikes in right & left foot lead
6. Moro-Moro Heaven Six Strikes in right & left foot lead
7. Moro-Moro Heaven & Earth Six Strikes in right & left foot lead
8. Moro-Moro Heaven & Earth Six Strikes in right & left foot lead
9. Moro-Moro Heaven Six Strikes in right and left foot lead
10. Prefix No.9 "Saboy" Strike Cadena Real in right foot lead
11. Combate General Clockwise Cadena Real & Prefix Earth Six in right & left foot lead
12. Combate General Counterclockwise Cadena Real & Prefix Earth Six in left & right foot lead
13. Magbabayo Redonda, Aldabis sa Ilalim in right & left foot lead
14. Moro-Moro Heaven Six Strikes in right & left foot lead
15. "X" Block, "Hook" Disarm Against No.1 "Taga" Strike in right foot lead
16. "X" Block "Hook" Disarm Against No.2 "Bartical" Strike in right foot lead
17. Heaven Six in right foot lead
18. Avalanche Doble in right foot lead

1. Kop-Kop High & Kop-Kop Low in right foot lead
2. Kop-Kop High & Kop-Kop Low in left foot lead
3. Prefix Downward Figure Eight Abecedario High, Low, High in right foot lead
4. Prefix Downward Figure Eight Abecedario High, Low, High in left foot lead
5. Prefix Moro-Moro Heaven Eight Strikes in right & left foot lead
6. Prefix Moro-Moro Heaven Eight Strikes in right & left foot lead
7. Prefix Moro-Moro Heaven & Earth Eight Strikes in right & left foot lead
8. Prefix Moro-Moro Heaven & Earth Eight Strikes in right & left foot lead
9. Prefix Moro-Moro Heaven Eight Strikes in right & left foot lead
10. Prefix No.9 "Saboy" Strike Cadena Real in right foot lead
11. Combate General Clockwise Cadena Real & Prefix Cola De Largarto in right & left foot lead
12. Combate General Counterclockwise Cadena Real & Prefix Cola De Largarto in left & right foot lead
13. Magbabayo Redonda, Aldabis sa Ilalim in right & left foot lead
14. Prefix Moro-Moro Heaven Eight Strikes in right & left foot lead
15. Inside "X" Block "Hook" Disarm Against No.3 "Kabas Kanon" Strike in right foot lead
16. Inside "X" Block "Hook" Disarm Against No.4 "Kabas Kaliwa" Strike in right foot lead
17. Heaven Six in right foot lead
18. Avalanche Doble in right foot lead

LINE DRILL #4

1. Kop-Kop High & Kop-Kop Low in right foot lead
2. Kop-Kop High & Kop-Kop Low in left foot lead
3. Prefix Abecedario High, Low, High in right foot lead
4. Prefix Abecedario High, Low, High in left foot lead
5. Redonda Heaven Six Strikes in right & left foot lead
6. Redonda Heaven Six Strikes in right & left foot lead
7. Redonda Heaven & Earth Six Strikes in right & left foot lead
8. Redonda Heaven & Earth Six Strikes in right & left foot lead
9. Redonda Heaven Six Strikes in right & left foot lead
10. Prefix No.1 "Taga" Strike Cadena Real in right foot lead
11. Combate General Clockwise Cadena Real & Metamorphosis Twelve in right & left foot lead
12. Combate General Counterclockwise Cadena Real & Metamorphosis Twelve in left & right foot lead
13. Magbabayo Redonda, Aldabis sa Ilalim in right & left foot lead
14. Redonda Heaven Six Strikes in right & left foot lead
15. "Cane" Disarm Against No.1 "Taga" Strike in right foot lead
16. "Cane" Disarm Against No.2 "Bartical" Strike in right foot lead
17. Heaven Six in right foot lead
18. Avalanche Doble in right foot lead

LINE DRILL #5

1. Kop-Kop High & Kop-Kop Low in right foot lead
2. Kop-Kop High & Kop-Kop Low in left foot lead
3. Prefix Redonda Abecedario High, Low, High in right foot lead
4. Prefix Redonda Abecedario High, Low, High in left foot lead
5. Prefix Redonda Heaven Ten Strikes in right & left foot lead
6. Prefix Redonda Heaven Ten Strikes in right & left foot lead
7. Prefix Redonda Heaven & Earth Ten Strikes in right &left foot lead
8. Prefix Redonda Heaven & Earth Ten Strikes in right & left foot lead
9. Prefix Redonda Planchada Heaven Ten Strikes in right & left foot lead
10. Prefix No.3 "Kabos Kanon" Strike Cadena Real in right foot lead
11. Combate General Clockwise Cadenda Real & Prefix Planchada Abierto in right & left foot lead
12. Combate General Counterclockwise Cadena Real & Prefix Plancada Abierto in left & right foot lead
13. Magbabayo Redonda, Aldabis sa Ilalim Strikes in right & left foot lead
14. Prefix Redonda Heaven Ten Strikes in right & left foot lead
15. "Cane" Disarm Against No.3 "Kabas Kanon" Strike in right foot lead
16. "Cane" Disarm Against No.4 "Kabas Kaliwa" Strike in left foot lead
17. Heaven Six in right foot lead
18. Avalanche Doble in right foot lead

LINE DRILL #6

1. Kop-Kop High, Kop-Kop Middle & Kop-Kop Low in right foot lead
2. Kop-Kop High, Kop-Kop Middle & Kop-Kop Low in left foot lead
3. Prefix Saboy Abecedario High, Low, High in right foot lead
4. Prefix Saboy Abecedario High, Low, High in left foot lead
5. Rapido Redonda Heaven Ten Strikes in right & left foot lead
6. Rapido Redonda Heaven Ten Strikes in right & left foot lead
7. Rapido Redonda Heaven & Earth Ten Strikes in right & left foot lead
8. Rapido Redonda Heaven & Earth Ten Strikes in right & left foot lead
9. Rapido Redonda Heaven Ten Strikes in right & left foot lead
10. Prefix No.1 "Taga" Strike Cadena Real in right foot lead
11. Combate General Clockwise Cadena Real & Prefix Redonda High in right & left foot lead
12. Combate General Counterclockwise Cadena Real & Prefix Redonda High in left & right foot lead
13. Magbabayo Redonda, Aldabis sa Ilalim in right & left foot lead
14. Rapido Redonda Heaven Ten Strikes in right & left foot lead
15. "Vine" Disarm Against No.3 "Kabas Kanon" Strike in right foot lead
16. "Vine" Disarm Against No.4 "Kabas Kaliwa" Strike in left foot lead
17. Heaven Six in left foot lead
18. Avalanche Doble in left foot lead

LINE DRILL #7

1. **Feeder & Receiver:** RFL & LFL Kop-Kop High, Middle & Low

2. **Receiver & Receiver:** RFL & LFL No.1 "Taga" & No.2 "Bartical" & No.3 "Kabos Kanon" & No.4 "Kabos Kaliwa" No.9 "Saboy" & No.8 "Aldabis"

3. **Feeder:** RFL Abecedario High, Low, High
   Receiver: RFL Heaven & Earth Six

4. **Feeder:** LFL Abecedario High, Low, High
   Receiver: LFL Heaven & Earth Six

5. **Feeder:** RFL & LFL Kali Six
   Receiver: RFL & LFL Heaven Six

6. **Feeder:** RFL & LFL Heaven Six
   Receiver: RFL & LFL Kali Six

7. **Feeder:** RFL & LFL Kali Six
   Receiver: RFL & LFL Heaven Six

8. **Feeder:** RFL & LFL Heaven & Earth Six
   Receiver: RFL & LFL Abecedario High, Low, High

9. **Feeder:** RFL Abecedario High, Low, High
   Receiver: RFL Heaven & Earth Six

10. **Feeder:** RFL Prefix No.1 "Taga" Strike Cadena Real
    Receiver: No.1 "Taga" Strike

11. **Feeder:** Combate General Clockwise Cadena Real & Prefix Heaven Six RFL &LFL

Receiver: Kali Six

12. **Feeder:** Combate General Counterclockwise Cadena Real & Prefix Heaven Six LFL & RFL **Receiver:** Kali Six

13. **Feeder:** RFL & LFL Prefix & Suffix Heaven Eight Strikes
    Receiver: RFL & LFL Prefix & Suffix Heaven Eight Strikes

14. **Feeder:** RFL & LFL Heaven Six Strikes
    Receiver: RFL & LFL Kali Six

15. **Feeder:** RFL Inside "Vine" Disarm Against No.1 "Taga" Strike
    Receiver: RFL No.1 "Taga" Strike

16. **Feeder:** RFL Inside "Hook" Disarm Against No.2 "Bartical" Strike
    Receiver: RFL No.2"Bartical' Strike

17. **Feeder:** RFL Heaven Six
    Receiver: Stands Accepts Strikes

18. **Feeder:** RFL Avalanche Doble
    Receiver: Stands Accepts Strikes

1. **Feeder:** RFL Prefix Abecedario High, Low, High
   Receiver: RFL Prefix Heaven & Earth Six

2. **Feeder:** LFL Prefix Abecedario High, Low, High
   Receiver: LFL Prefix Heaven & Earth Six

3. **Feeder:** RFL & LFL Prefix Kali Six
   Receiver: RFL & LFL Prefix Heaven Six

4. **Feeder:** RFL & LFL Prefix Heaven Six
   Receiver: RFL & LFL Prefix Kali Six

5. **Feeder:** RFL & LFL Prefix Kali Six
   Receiver: RFL & LFL Prefix Heaven Six

6. **Feeder:** RFL & LFL Prefix Heaven & Earth Six
   Receiver: RFL & LFL Prefix Abecedario High, Low, High

7. **Feeder:** RFL Prefix Abecedario High, Low, High
   Receiver: RFL Prefix Heaven & Earth Six

8. **Feeder:** RFL Prefix No.1 "Taga" Strike Cadena Real
   Receiver: No.1 "Taga" Strike

9. **Feeder:** Combate General Clockwise Cadena Real & Prefix Earth Six RFL &LFL
   Receiver: Kali Six

10. **Feeder:** Combate General Counterclockwise Cadena Real & Prefix Earth Six LFL & RFL
    Receiver: Kali Six

11. **Feeder:** RFL & LFL Prefix & Suffix Heaven Eight Strikes
    Receiver: RFL & LFL Prefix & Suffix Heaven Eight Strikes

12. **Feeder:** RFL & LFL Heaven Six Strikes
    Receiver: RFL & LFL Kali Six

13. **Feeder:** RFL Inside "Vine" Disarm Against No.3 "Kabas Kanon" Strike
    Receiver: RFL No.3 "Kabas Kanon" Strike

14. **Feeder:** LFL Inside "Vine" Disarm Against No.4 "Kabas Kaliwa" Strike
    Receiver: LFL No.4 "Kabas Kaliwa" Strike

15. **Feeder:** LFL Heaven Six
    Receiver: Stands Accepts Strikes

16. **Feeder:** LFL Avalanche Doble
    Receiver: Stands Accepts Strikes

1. **Feeder:** RFL Prefix Redondo Abecedario High, Low, High
Receiver: RFL Prefix Heaven & Earth Six

2. **Feeder:** LFL Prefix Redondo Abecedario High, Low, High
Receiver: LFL Prefix Heaven & Earth Six

3. **Feeder:** RFL & LFL Prefix Redondo Kali Six
Receiver: RFL & LFL Prefix Redondo Heaven Six

4. **Feeder:** RFL & LFL Prefix Redondo Heaven Six
Receiver: RFL & LFL Prefix Redondo Kali Six

5. **Feeder:** RFL & LFL Prefix Redondo Kali Six
Receiver: RFL & LFL Prefix Redondo Heaven Six

6. **Feeder:** RFL & LFL Prefix Redondo Heaven & Earth Six
Receiver: RFL & LFL Prefix Redondo Abecedario High, Low, High

7. **Feeder:** RFL Prefix Redondo Abecedario High, Low, High
Receiver: RFL Prefix Redondo Heaven & Earth Six

8. **Feeder:** RFL Prefix Redondo No.1 Strike Cadena Real
Receiver: Prefix Redondo No.1 "Taga" Strike

9. **Feeder:** Combate General Clockwise Cadena Real & Prefix Redondo Earth Six RFL &LFL
Receiver: Prefix Redondo Kali Six Low

10. **Feeder:** Combate General Counterclockwise Cadena Real & Prefix Redondo Earth Six LFL & RFL **Receiver:** Prefix Redondo Kali Six Low

11. **Feeder:** RFL & LFL Prefix & Suffix Heaven Eight Strikes

Receiver: RFL & LFL Prefix & Suffix Heaven Eight Strikes

12. **Feeder:** RFL & LFL Prefix Redondo Heaven Six Strikes
Receiver: RFL & LFL Prefix Redondo Kali Six High

13. **Feeder:** RFL Inside Crusada Disarm Against No.3 "Kabas Kanon" Strike
Receiver: RFL No.3 "Kabas Kaliwa" Strike

14. **Feeder:** LFL Inside Crusada Disarm Against No.4 "Kabas Kaliwa" Strike
Receiver: LFL No.4 "Kabas Kaliwa" Strike

15. **Feeder:** LFL Heaven Six
Receiver: Stands Accepts Strikes

16. **Feeder:** LFL Avalanche Doble
Receiver: Stands Accepts Strikes

LINE DRILL #10

1. **Feeder:** RFL Prefix Kop-Kop, Redondo Abecedario High, Low, High
   Receiver: RFL Prefix Kop-Kop, Redondo, Heaven & Earth Six

2. **Feeder:** LFL Prefix Kop-Kop, Redondo, Heaven & Earth Six
   Receiver: LFL Prefix Kop-Kop, Redondo, Heaven & Earth Six

3. **Feeder:** RFL & LFL Prefix Redondo Kali Six
   Receiver: RFL & LFL Prefix Redondo Heaven Six

4. **Feeder:** RFL & LFL Prefix Redondo Heaven Six
   Receiver: RFL & LFL Prefix Redondo Kali Six

5. **Feeder:** RFL & LFL Prefix Redondo Kali Six
   Receiver: RFL & LFL Prefix Redondo Heaven Six

6. **Feeder:** RFL & LFL Prefix Redondo Heaven & Earth Six
   Receiver: RFL & LFL Prefix Redondo Abecedario High, Low, High

7. **Feeder:** RFL Prefix Redondo Abecedario High, Low, High
   Receiver: RFL Prefix Redondo Heaven & Earth Six

8. **Feeder:** RFL Prefix Redondo No.1 "Taga" Strike Cadena Real
   Receiver: Prefix Redondo No.1 "Taga" Strike

9. **Feeder:** Combate General Clockwise Cadena Real & Prefix Kop-Kop, Redondo Heaven & Earth Six RFL &LFL
   Receiver: Prefix Kop-Kop, Redondo Kali Six High, Low

10. **Feeder:** Combate General Counterclockwise Cadena Real & Prefix Kop-Kop, Redondo Heaven & Earth Six LFL & RFL
    Receiver: Prefix Kop-Kop, Redondo Kali Six High, Low

11. **Feeder:** RFL & LFL Prefix & Suffix Heaven Eight Strikes
    Receiver: RFL & LFL Prefix & Suffix Heaven Eight Strikes

12. **Feeder:** RFL & LFL Prefix Redondo Heaven Six Strikes
    Receiver: RFL & LFL Prefix Redondo Kali Six High

13. **Feeder:** RFL to LFL Outside Crusada Disarm Against No.1 "Taga" Strike
    Receiver: RFL No.1 "Taga" Strike

14. **Feeder:** LFL to RFL Outside Crusada Disarm Against No.2 "Bartical" Strike
    Receiver: LFL No.2 "Bartical" Strike

15. **Feeder:** RFL Heaven Six
    Receiver: Stands Accepts Strikes

16. **Feeder:** RFL Avalanche Doble
    Receiver: Stands Accepts Strikes

GLOSSARY: OTHER EXPRESSIONS USED IN ESCRIMA FROM THE NORTHERN, CENTRAL AND SOUTHERN REGIONS OF THE PHILIPPINES.

A

Abanico – Fanning motion
Abierta – Open guard position (forehand)
Agaw/Desarma –Disarm
Amarra – Striking pattern / fighting combination or Strike
Ankab-Pagkusi / Kinomutai – Biting & pinching
Anyo / Sayaw / Forma / Modelo – Set form
Arco – Rainbow Arcing strike or Romantic expression for new beginnings

B

Bangkaw – Spear
Bartical/Diagonal – Angular Strike

C

Cadena – Chain
Corto – Close Range fighting
Curbada /Arco / Encorvada – Curving strike like a wild five strike

D

Daga / Baraw / Cuchillo – Dagger / knife
De Fondo – To anchor or plant oneself
Doble Olisi / Baston – Double stick
Dungab / Sak-Sak / Clavada –Thrust
Dumog / Buno / Kulubutt – Filipino Grappling

E

Enganos – Faking

Entablado – a fixed routine or staged performance
Escrimador – A practitioner of Escrima
Escuda -Shield Abecedario – Basic block & counter A, B, C's high, low, high
Espada y Daga – Sword & Dagger
Estilo de Salon – quick rhythmical footwork or dancing style
Estocada – Long blade drills

G

Gunting – Scissors
Gununting – Scissor motion
Guro – Teacher/Instructor

H

Hagbong / Bagsak / Tajada / Corta Bajo – Cut down or slice down
Hampak / Tero / Armarra / Punetazo – To hit
Hayang – Open / palm up
Higot/Atada / Cuerda – To tie
Hubud/Desatada / De Cuerda – To untie

I

Ilag Paa / Paseos – footwork

J

Juego Todo / Vale Todo – Full contact, no holds bar fight, or "Estilo de Matador"

K

Kali(s) / Baraw – Sword & Dagger
Kamot – Body or hand motion (as in KA-li)
Kaw-it/Recortada – Clipping
Kulob – Closed / palm down
Kunsi/Armbar – Lock / Submission

L

Laban Handa – Ready stance position
Labtik – To hit through the target
Largo – Long Range fighting
Lihok – Motion (as in ka-LI)
Likos / Puter kepala – Circle throw
Lubud /Mezclada – To blend
Luton – Flow (drill) or footwork

M

Mandirigma – Warrior's stance in a back stance position
Matador – Killer or reference to a fight to the death
Media – Middle
Medio – Medium range fighting

O

Olisi / Baston / Palo - Stick
Oliso Palad / Tabak Maliit – Pocket stick / palm stick
Ordabis – Backfist

P

Paglibot – Round kick
Pakal / Lupa – Ice-pick grip (knife)
Palasut / Seguida – To pass
Panastas / Contra – To slash against

Pangamot – Unarmed fighting or empty hands fighting
Panantukan – Filipino boxing
Patuyok – Twirling like in redonda
Payong – Umbrella
Pinga – Short Staff
Pingki-Pingki – Double weapon coordination drills
Plansa / Planchada – Horizontal
Primero – Strike held at target (Beginners)
Punyo – Butt of weapon
Punta – Point of weapon

R

Redondo – Tightening circular strike / Flywheel
Retirado – To retreat

S

Sabayan /Combate Fuerza – Simultaneous attacks or attack by combination
Sablet – Quick release (disarm)
Sak-Sak / Langit – Hammer / sabre grip (knife)
Saka / Corta Arriba / Aldabis – Cut up
Serrada – Closed guard position (backhand)
Sibat – Long Staff
Sikaran – Filipino Karate
Siko / Codo – Elbow
Sikod – Push kick
Siko-Siko – Trident (Sai)
Sinawali – an interweaving pattern, woven
Sipa – Low stomp / oblique kick
Sonkete / Picada – Poking thrusting strike
Sumbrada / Contra Sumbrada – Counter for Counter or Roof Block
Sungab – Finger thrust or spear hand

T

Tabak Toyok – Flail (Nunchaku)
Tapi/Parry – Checking
Tenedor – Fork or Filipino Romantic Expression for Split entry
Tresello / Kia – Lobtik, Witik, Lobtik motion
Tuhod / Rodilla – Knee
Tuo / Derecho – Right

W

Wala / Izquierda – Left
Witik / Kia / Contra Compas – Snap hit or strike